SHAPED BY WIND
AND WATER

THE *CREDO* SERIES

A *credo* is a statement of belief, an assertion of deep conviction. The *Credo* series offers contemporary American writers whose work emphasizes the natural world and the human community the opportunity to discuss their essential goals, concerns, and practices. Each volume presents an individual writer's *credo,* his or her investigation of what it means to write about human experience and society in the context of the more-than-human world, as well as a biographical profile and complete bibliography of the author's published work. The *Credo* series offers some of our best writers an opportunity to speak to the fluid and subtle issues of rapidly changing technology, social structure, and environmental conditions.

SHAPED BY WIND AND WATER

REFLECTIONS OF A NATURALIST

ANN HAYMOND ZWINGER

Scott Slovic, *Credo* Series Editor

Credo

MILKWEED EDITIONS

Published 2000 by Milkweed Editions
Printed in Canada
Cover illustration by Ann Haymond Zwinger, courtesy of Hedgebrook,
a retreat for women writers on Whidbey Island (www.hedgebrook.org).
Interior illustrations by Ann Haymond Zwinger
Cover design by Gail Wallinga
Author photo by Sid Dobrin
The text of this book is set in Stone Serif.
00 01 02 03 04   5 4 3 2 1
First Edition

Milkweed Editions, a nonprofit publisher, gratefully acknowledges
support from our World As Home Funders: Lila-Wallace Reader's
Digest Fund; Creation and Presentation Programs of the National
Endowment for the Arts; and Elly Sturgis. Other support has been
provided by the Elmer L. and Eleanor J. Andersen Foundation; James
Ford Bell Foundation; Bush Foundation; General Mills Foundation;
Honeywell Foundation; Jerome Foundation; McKnight Foundation;
Minnesota State Arts Board through an appropriation by the
Minnesota State Legislature; Norwest Foundation on behalf of
Norwest Bank Minnesota, Norwest Investment Management and
Trust, Lowry Hill, Norwest Investment Services, Inc.; Lawrence and
Elizabeth Ann O'Shaughnessy Charitable Income Trust in honor
of Lawrence M. O'Shaughnessy; Oswald Family Foundation; Ritz
Foundation on behalf of Mr. and Mrs. E. J. Phelps Jr.; John and
Beverly Rollwagen Fund of the Minneapolis Foundation; St. Paul
Companies, Inc.; Star Tribune Foundation; Dayton's, Mervyn's, and
Target Stores by the Target Foundation; U.S. Bancorp Piper Jaffray
Foundation on behalf of U.S. Bancorp Piper Jaffray; and generous
individuals.

Library of Congress Cataloging-in-Publication Data

Zwinger, Ann.
  Shaped by wind and water : reflections of a naturalist / Ann
  Haymond Zwinger.— 1st ed.
    p. cm. — (Credo)
  Includes bibliographical references (p.).
    ISBN 1-57131-241-2 (cloth) — ISBN 1-57131-240-4 (pbk.)
    I. Natural history—Authorship. 2. Zwinger, Ann. I. Title.
  II. Credo (Minneapolis, Minn.)

QH14.Z95 2000
508—dc21   99-055767

To my mother, Helen Louise Glass, and to my sister Jane

And to all the wonderful women in my life,
understanding that more than one category
generally applies to each:
mothers, daughters, friends, colleagues,
aunts, and cousins, and to those
who reach into the future,
Sally Ann Roberts and Sarah Drummond
and my three river goddaughters:
Zöe Ackerman, Regina Ann Conley,
and Malia Ann Rivas-Tate

Shaped by Wind and Water

Shaped by Wind and Water: Reflections
of a Naturalist
by Ann Haymond Zwinger
First Morning   3
Second Morning   17
Third Morning   31
Fourth Morning   41
Fifth Morning   55
Sixth Morning   69
Last Morning   83

Ann Haymond Zwinger: A Portrait   87
by Scott Slovic

Bibliography of Ann Haymond Zwinger's Work   113
by Scott Slovic

Experto crede:
aliquid amplius in silvis
invenies quam in libris.
Ligna et lapides docubunt
te quod a magistris audire
non possis.

—St. Bernard of Clairvaux

SHAPED BY WIND
AND WATER

HEDGEBROOK · TIDE GOING OUT · DEER BAY 12·8·98

Shaped by Wind and Water

REFLECTIONS OF A NATURALIST

by Ann Haymond Zwinger

First Morning

> *I'm a little anxious. How am I to bring off this conception? Directly one gets to work one is like a person walking, who has seen the country stretching out before. I want to write nothing in this book that I don't enjoy writing. Yet writing is always difficult.*

> —Virginia Woolf

I stand in the middle of Oak Cottage, awash in indecision of where to begin. Oak Cottage is one of six small cottages at Hedgebrook, located on Whidbey Island in Puget Sound. Hedgebrook is a retreat for women writers (one of only two or three such retreats in the United States), where dedicated writers are fed and housed and can work without worrying about the usual necessities and responsibilities. Unbeknown to me on this first day is that Hedgebrook will become the frame for this book, and this cottage a blessedly solitary, beautifully ordered symbol of a cloistered and happy existence.

I am aware that I am the recipient of a generous and unexpected gift of uncluttered time, of a finite beginning and ending contained within these walls, beneath a slanted ceiling with its handsomely pegged beams, behind a sturdy door with its handmade ironwork, and the beveled panes of perfectly proportioned windows that fracture the light into colored spectra when the sun shines. Within this matrix I will come to have a sense of order, a recognition of beliefs, and a direction of prose. I have had extended periods of solitude in the desert and on islands; I've had river trips where I did not have to worry about planning or preparing the meals; I've had time away from telephones and doorbells and life's eternal interruptions. But never all three at once. Instead of juggling a life, I am faced with solitude and serenity and why I am here: to write, and *only* to write. Organizing *me* seems to be the biggest challenge. Like too much water on a parched soil, I can't absorb it all at once.

Many women I know live the same kind of life, predicated on interruption, that I do—the push-me/pull-me dance of balancing family life and professional life: keeping in touch with family, doing another wash, marketing and cooking, juggling overlapping schedules, and getting done what needs to be done. For a writer trying to find isolated unpeopled time to write, add the conflicts of trying to get a rough draft on paper and seeing friends; preparing for and attending various meetings, writing speeches, answering the multitudinous messages that come by voice mail, fax, E-mail, and post, and doing research; reading and evaluating manuscripts and honoring your own deadline. And I'm not even a single working mother with children to pick up from day care and help with homework and carry on the necessary tasks that consume thirty hours of the day.

When I began writing, I often railed against the unnecessary and incessant stoppages that clotted my day, insulted my deadlines. Writing, unlike needlepoint, is not something one can pick up and put down easily. Fieldwork and research and putting it together as natural history writing is, of necessity, time consuming. I am a foot-dragging writer, and the computer simply indulges my bad habit of producing an excessive number of drafts. I have never had the luxury of a set schedule and blocks of time to write, and, being pragmatic, I've learned to trust my mind's ability to work on its own, to explore ideas and mentally file and order them while I make a chocolate roll or sew on a button. I *do* know that blocks of time are necessary for many of the tasks of writing; I appreciate them when I have them and yearn for more. But I also could be persuaded that in a life of unavoidable interruptions there might be some hidden blessings: when I finally *do* have the chance to work, my mind immediately focuses in and expands my moment in the sunshine. The self-indulgence of "writer's block" is a luxury that never wrote an essay and, interestingly enough, something I seldom hear women writers complain about.

Certainly such a lifestyle demands self-discipline and the ability to shift mental gears quickly. I work best in the morning when my energy level is high, but morning is also the time that exercise and household activities get done. I must often use less productive times of the day to work, sure that some afternoon when my metabolism hits rock bottom, my head is going to fall forward on the keyboard and "e-r-t-y-u-i-o" will be permanently imprinted on my brow. I also take advantage of time in the air to do a great deal of editing; at thirty-five thousand feet on the way between hither and yon, no one so far can reach me on the telephone or ring my attention button. Besides, editing shortens the trip amazingly.

I thought I was prepared for feeling somewhat at sea in this new situation that Hedgebrook provides of beautiful, bountiful, unstructured time, but I am off-balance with the unfamiliarity. I believe in the good health of change, that new situations are necessary—teetering off-balance once in awhile keeps me in balance the rest of the while. But I'm bemused that I'm doing just what I thought I had rationalized myself out of doing: standing in the middle of the room, happily bewildered, facing an unbelievable day without end amen to do with as I wish. It is an amazing feeling. An absolutely *amazing* feeling.

When I arrived last night, amid driving rain, I had little idea what the cottage was like and, what's more, was too tired to care after a day of missed connections and prolonged, strapped-in sitting, trying to get from Colorado Springs to Seattle to the Mulkiteo Ferry to Whidbey Island. I walked off the ferry onto the island into an ultramarine evening full of rainy reflections, trying to manage an umbrella and luggage and miss the big puddles. Bev Graham, one of the gardeners on staff, picked me out of the line of plodding commuters and whisked me to Hedgebrook half an hour away.

I sat down to a warm, welcoming meal with six strangers, one of whom, Carolyn Servid, kindly walked me back to Oak Cottage by rainlight (that thoughtfulness would come to epitomize my time here in the company of lively, imaginative, and skilled professional writers). I didn't bother to unpack, just flopped into bed, a drylander absorbing the unaccustomed and lovely cadence of rain on a shake-shingle roof.

So not until I awoke this morning in a meager gray light was I able to orient myself to Oak Cottage. My bed almost fills the width of a loft that crosses the center of the cottage like a bridge. From the loft, framed by an open railing, I look down on one side to a worktable lighted by two corner windows and a small built-in kitchen with the requisite accessories. From the other side of the loft, steep ladder steps descend, paralleling a sloping roof that ends four feet off the ground, allowing room for three large square windows placed low under the eaves. They frame the boles of a small cluster of friendly eyed aspen to which a few late Naples yellow leaves still cling. Typical aspen: like slot machines, they tumble one yellow leaf, then two, then all three at once, the gold pours out, and then it's all over.

I dress and work my way slowly down the ladder in wool-socked feet, as yet unaccustomed to the steep pitch. Around the corner I find a bay with a window seat. An overstuffed chair. A floor lamp. A small bookcase with a thesaurus and dictionary, bird and tree identification books, and Anne Morrow Lindbergh's *Gift from the Sea*. A small sheepherder's stove provides the cottage's only source of heat.

Curious as to dimensions, I pace off the length of the cottage; the twenty-odd feet from wall to wall are a surprise, for the cottage strikes me as much larger because it's so spacious and airy. The cottages seem to grow out of the landscape. The huge hand-hewn oak beams that, tradition says, sing for seven years of the forest left behind, are secured by pegs. Elegant simplicity and fine craftsmanship, like the beveled windowpanes, typify this living space and establish for me a sense of psychological order, the respect of materials a statement in itself. That the cottage is mine alone to occupy absolutely adds to its charm.

I lay out pad and pencil on the worktable, lining up the edge of the pad with the edge of the table, just as I did as a child. I arrange my watercolor pens, taking pleasure just as I did as a child in following the sequence of color: scarlet, apricot, saffron, Naples yellow, grass green, olive green, ultramarine blue, lavender, dove gray. The arrangement of familiar working materials engenders a shift of mind, orients me to anticipate work to embark upon, drawings to consider, serendipitous times of looking and learning and absorbing, contemplating and coming to terms, the potential of creating, of following an assignment, of groping to find, examine, and come to terms with the credos by which I live.

Before this exercise, if someone had asked me to write down what I believe, I'm afraid I would have given a smart-ass reply: "Take two of my books and call me in the morning." My discomfort with intro-spection may be why I prefer natural history writing, which dictates an outward focus, not an inward one. I prefer recording in field notes what watching and waiting bring to pass, what fly swerves with verve, what kingfisher yatters about the summer, what gypsy rose flings away its petals and which cactus flower gathers in its tiny nectar-besotted bees and closes over them like a comforter for the night, what lizard scarfs up flies and what lizard siphons up ants, and what raven responds courteously when spoken to with civility. Asking me to focus inward and posit what I believe is asking this wandering, desultory, quiet-seeking, river-loving pebble collector to be-come a heavy metal groupie with a headset vibrating deafening bass sounds twenty-four hours a day.

For a writer allergic to the pontifical "I," running the rivers of the mind is much more dangerous than being pummeled by rapids on actual rivers. But, as a friend pointed out to me, the heartening thing about introspection is that one embarks on new paths through old forests, and often finds trees caparisoned with new species of lichen and moss, punctuated with unfamiliar mushrooms as well as familiar confirmations and realizations, plus the comfortable appreciation of beliefs that have held up over time like good hiking boots. And naturally one finds some rubbish that needs to be packed up and carried out to the nearest trash can, like petty concerns, useless worries, bad tempers, depression, and one's delusions of virtue.

In my wanderings I am to rediscover that peculiar truth known to bird-watchers: sometimes the only way to see an elusive singer in the foliage is to look at the larger pattern of leaves and branches in a peripheral way, and suddenly the bird pops into view. I will find in the following of my daily routine at Hedgebrook that—ah HAH!—beliefs *do* pop into focus, clearly visible and full of color.

I am very aware of operating on a set of principles and values, inculcated by culture, by parents, by my own pragmatic/idealistic views of what is right and fitting and proper and civil. Although they underlie how I live, I don't give much thought to them unless provoked by questions as to their existence. If I stopped and raided my moral stores for every decision I made, I'd exist in a constant morass of indecision: the difference between right and wrong is straightforward; it is the decision between two rights that keeps me awake at night.

I admit, with reluctance, that pulling these beliefs,

kicking and screaming, out of a corner of my brain into consciousness is probably a worthy activity that one should do every so often, like cleaning out the refrigerator or winnowing out closets. It may rank right up there with cleaning up my impossibly messy workroom, catching up on three-year-old correspondence, writing a first draft, having a root canal, and filing. I assume I'll feel better when it's over.

I must also admit, at the beginning, that I am a hopelessly pedantic, pragmatic, practical American citizen, flatly middle class, WASP: that is, a white Anglo-Saxon pantheist. But one needs to begin with who and where one is to understand where one might possibly be going.

Very simply, I believe a sun-warmed beach pebble, held tightly enough in my hand to feel its pulse, tells me about its geological underpinnings, tells me what it is like to be shaped by water, tells me all I need to know in its elegant beauty of form.

A sudden shiver reminds me the cottage may be mine alone, but it's also chilly. I dig out my thermometer (naturalists always carry thermometers): fifty-eight degrees. I build a fire and stuff too much wood into the small stove box. The stove responds by teaching me its first lesson: patience. The fire goes out and a wisp of bitter smoke snakes into the room.

I begin again, putting in one crumpled newspaper upon which I carefully lay three pieces of kindling. This time I wait until the kindling burns cheerfully, add a small piece of wood, wait for it to catch before putting in another. As the stove sighs and ticks and begins to warm the space around it, I am transported back in time to the years of cooking on a woodstove at Constant Friendship, our place in the mountains. I always thought that in summertime a woodstove was a nuisance—I didn't welcome the woodstove's by-product of excess heat on a hot day, and I would have preferred to have been out hiking or drawing. But in wintertime a woodstove comes into its own.

The date on my Colorado mountain stove is 1906; the name emblazoned on its brow, Lowell-Meserve, was a well-known hardware store in Colorado at the turn of the century. The stove sits solid and firm on four clawed feet, its bulk reassuring, its dignity immense, an elegant old dowager in black silk holding court on a Florentine afternoon. A bosomy warming oven leans out over the top of the stove, fitted with a roll-down cover where I can dry pinned insect specimens safe from marauding spiders. The stovepipe runs up through it, providing the kind of gentle heat that warms ice-cold plates and raises bread. But the stove could also be a harridan, hissing odorous fumes out of every indignant crack, and I got the message in unmistakable terms when I was clumsy and inept and hasty, as I was this morning. It knew (and so did I) that if necessary, it could warm the whole world.

No fancy directions come with a woodstove, and no cookbook. One learns on the job, through a scorched hand-and-thigh policy, an occasional dazzling success, and coming to terms. It took me much too long to remember that the entire stove gets hot, including the coiled-wire oven-door handle that left burn stripes on my palm. In effect, the whole top of a woodstove is a burner, although the fire burns only beneath the firebox on the right side. Whenever drops of condensation from the tin roof fell on it, they registered in a patois of hisses. A woodstove is more than a device for cooking. It is a learning process in which one learns as much about oneself as about cooking, and in so doing, acquires patience, respect, affection, and tact. Cooking on a woodstove deals in the basics of life, nourishment and companionship, warmth, family, and friends.

In the early days at Constant Friendship, cooking on the woodstove may have blistered my thighs, but the uninsulated floor remained icy, and I fervently hoped that the pump wouldn't freeze up before the dishes were done. Somewhere along the way we added a reservoir in which heating water sounded like a giant's borborygmus. Plentiful hot water made dish washing a pleasure, and washing dishes by hand is a task that belongs on my "busy-hands syndrome" list. I believe that there are some common, familiar occupations, like preparing meals or dish washing, that, as they engage the hands, unlock the head and make possible wonderful, worthwhile, vintage communications between participants, conversation that simply doesn't occur otherwise or elsewhere.

Off and on for the past thirty years we have cooked the Thanksgiving turkey in that woodstove. A woodstove toasts every square millimeter of bird to a perfect golden brown, better than any modern stove does. Some years we dragged food on a sled for a mile because snow was too deep to drive through; sometimes the wind lifted the napkins off the table inside; sometimes the sky gathered itself together in huge clouds pregnant with winter. And sometimes the sun shone and our footsteps crunched through crisp leaves on a starched, seemingly September day.

Thanksgiving is far and away my favorite holiday: you're not obligated to purchase, wrap, create, dress up, or observe a jump-through-the-hoop list of societal expectations. Thanksgiving is a surcease from all that. In addition, the quiet pause of the day prompts us to take stock of the good things piled up during the year, to hug family and friends, to cook and eat food that nourishes the heart and head as well as the body, to count snowflakes sifting down against a black lake or measure the ice that covers it, to search for the one last yellow aspen leaf that has escaped the season. Everyone contributes to such a day, from the eight-month-old (who helps by sleeping soundly at dinner-time) to eight-year-old Sally Ann, who makes place cards, to the eighty-year-old who rolls up sleeves and whomps up a pint of whipped cream.

Traditionally we join hands and stand in a circle to say what each of us is thankful for. The words are no litany of successes and achievements, but a more somber recognition of the deeper gifts of life: good health, dear friends, ample food, a roof over our heads, worthwhile work to do. There is an underlying seriousness in what we say, that in caring for this time and this place we foster our capacity to care for a larger time and larger place, and that we do not bear our accountability lightly. When so much in the world about us seems so awry, the sturdy warmth that radiates from the stove and the peacefulness of the landscape outside reminds us where we are: we are humans, we are thankful, and we are blessed.

Swathed in pleasant memories, I watch the flames in the little sheepherder's stove waver and dart. I shut the door and tap the damper near to closed and reflect that the rewards of a woodstove may far outweigh its demands. I like feeling a part of all the women who have heated and cooked on woodstoves, knowing that they too cajoled and cursed, jiggled the firebox handle impatiently to drop the ashes through, moved the coffee two inches to the left to perk more slowly, and turned out food that their children still speak of with nostalgia, a still-open circle, a continuity of past and present.

When I walk up to the woodshed to replenish my supply, I find Barton Cole there, stacking fresh-cut wood. Barton is another of the three gardeners, Cathy Breummer being the third. The gardeners cut and stack wood twice a year, a three-day-or-more job. They cut newly delivered logs into stove lengths with a chain saw, then split them with a mechanical splitter, toss the resultant heap onto the truck, and haul it up here to the woodshed, where the wood is dumped again into another disorganized heap. All three feel, time consuming and labor intensive as the job may be, there's an irreplaceable sense of satisfaction in doing it.

When I admire the ten-foot-high facade of the newly risen woodpile, Barton says with some pride, "You don't just *stack* wood, you *place* it." Barton's tone befits a Distinguished Research Fellow with the American Society of Crows and Ravens. The ends of the fresh-cut wood in the wall behind him, a right angle joined by a curve, nestle against each other to form unexpected patterns of serpentines and spirals and swirls. The stacked wood is a handsome creation in its unconscious interplay of natural forms and colors, the dark interstices setting off the arcs of the growth rings.

In that pleasant moment, the relationship between earth and tree, cutter and stacker, my stove and me, is crystal clear. Because of one tree's growth I stay comfortable. Because of someone else's labor I stay warm. From this earth I receive my daily heat, my daily comfort, my prayer of wood. Here, at this moment, I believe, without any doubt, that I am part of a continuum that begins with a sprouted seed and ends with warmth.

Second Morning

We are looking for a tongue that speaks with reverence for life, searching for an ecology of mind. Without it, we have no home, have no place of our own within the creation.

—Linda Hogan

In the rising light of morning I stand at the sink, mesmerized by the plethora of greenery that fills the window frame, eating toast so liberally slathered with honey that over the sink seems the only sensible place to eat it. Frondlike greenery, richly branched trees, waist-high bracken at the edge of the woods, spidery evergreen huckleberries, all with multiple multiplex leaves, small to minute, clad branches and stems even in winter.

Raindrops silver the scales of the cedar boughs. When the wind gusts, the branch tips gyrate and inscribe ovals in a giddy, hysterical dance. They remind me of an old film in which a director gave Picasso a light-tipped wand in a dark room and said, "Draw!" Picasso made those same eloquent, sweeping circles and ellipses, movements from the shoulder, an aerial calligraphy as distinctive as handwriting, and as hypnotic to watch, grandiose Möbius loops scribed into thin air.

These woods are so different from the open-floored ponderosa pine woods with which I am familiar in Colorado. Here thick undergrowth flourishes beneath the trees, giving the whole forest of cedars, firs, and Douglas firs a dense and somber aspect. While the growth of most trees is regulated by day length, red cedars respond to warmth, and photosynthesize even on short, sunny winter days. Unlike other conifers, red cedars self-fertilize and produce fertile cones and seeds even in poor years. The specific name for red cedar, *plicata,* refers to the way in which the leaves appear pleated onto the stem in such a way that the entire branch offers as large an area as possible to the sunlight—a scarce commodity here, it seems to me. The tiny scales that form the leaves of a red cedar fascinate me—how they're arranged, the intricate pairings and overlappings, the kindly claspings and imbrications, so that when the branch is all assembled, it bows gently, gracefully. I am dismayed to realize that, as a writer, I will consume one of these gorgeous trees a year for paper to feed my habit. I am more horrified when I consider the unmitigated wastefulness of the junk mail that clutters my desk.

Red cedars usually grow in mixed stands as they do here in this third-growth forest—Whidbey Island has been almost totally logged twice. I am appalled to read that, when old-growth forests are cut, despite claims of tree farm replacement advocates, what has been lost in the cutting may be impossible to regain. The centuries-old trees supported in their canopies a rich and diverse population of arthropods, salamanders, insects, and rodents, as well as a huge microscopic flora of yeasts and bacteria. The development of such an elaborate flora and fauna requires at least decades, more likely centuries. This quality and quantity of hangers-on separates older forests from the younger monoculture trees planted in rows on tree farms (which, incidently, do not produce wood as strong as the old growth they replace because they grow faster and have wider annual rings, good mostly only for paper products). In these farmed trees there are no fat lettuce lichens, no numerous fungi that produce insect-killing compounds, no wealth of bats that roost in rotten tree tops. They lack the advantages of the epiphytes that contribute nitrogen to their growth and absorb moisture from fog and rainfall, or the fungal partners that are toxic to insects. When old growth is cut, it takes down with it all the interconnected lives of plants and animals that exist in this incredibly rich, canopied world, vibrating and elaborate interrelationships that hold a world together.

I stand by the sink, intensely engaged with the flickering green outside the window. A quick movement on the ground barely catches my eye, hardly even a shadow, a small lump of brown earth changing space from a clump of bracken to a heap of windfall. Another winter wren!

I had never seen a winter wren until yesterday, when I made the introductory tour of Hedgebrook's woods with Barton. An excellent naturalist, he reeled off the names of trees and shrubs and mushrooms until I yearned for paper and pencil to write and sketch this abundance of natural history detail into memory.

In the midst of his litany, a movement, not color, caught my eye, a small something that materialized into a bird that moved briskly, through and under fallen branches, prodding and poking at dead leaves and twigs. I tiptoed after it, expecting it to take flight, or at least to disappear. Instead it bustled along, unconcerned by my scrutiny, too busy to bother with observers, lifting and sifting and jabbing for insects in the debris that accrues on a northwestern forest floor. Bustly little creature, rotund of body, short tailed, self-contained. I whispered "wren" without exactly knowing why, then added "winter?" That unsuspected identity must have been drawn from a pattern in some mental file drawer listing the combined characteristics of small, engrossed ground feeder with dark feathers, winter active.

Without a name I can learn nothing about the current object of my affection. It greatly satisfies something in my untidy nature to know that I watched *Troglodytes troglodytes,* and to know its name comes from the Greek meaning a creeper into holes or a cave dweller. And to find out that while there are nine species of wrens in North America, winter wrens are the only wren species in Europe. In many parts of North America, they are the winter-long singing members of the forest—Thoreau heard its "incessant lisping tinkle" in the mountains of New Hampshire.

A name also defines what is not as well as what is. A wren is not a red-winged blackbird and the why is as interesting as the fact. Now I can look up wrens in general and this one in particular. Maybe I'll even find one of those captivating connections that so delight devotees of natural history, feel a delectable sense of satisfaction, smile out loud, feel better about the hour.

Unfamiliar as these woods were, they became on the instant "home." A place where I knew somebody's name, not as something to check off on a trophy list but a handle on finding out something about it. Yes, I recognized the hallmark hemlock and red cedar, Douglas fir and bigleaf maple because Susan, my eldest daughter who lives on Whidbey Island, taught me. But it was that self-absorbed, officiously energetic little wren that gave me welcome. Given that I scarcely knew a wren from a wrench from a wench from a winch thirty years ago, when I started writing, I draw enormous pleasure from what has been added to my life.

Answering the question "What is that?" means that, over time, one builds a vocabulary of names, an activity which may sound about as exciting as watching pudding set. But not to this taxonomical devotee. I believe in knowing the names of things, the assigning of which is such a human necessity. Taxonomy allows me to access a massive body of knowledge. A name is a pathway to getting acquainted. Only then I can find out how a Douglas fir responds to the wind storm or the summer hail, how it grows and how it whispers, how it gets along in the world, how it values its habitat. In the near foreseeable future, when I shall become one of their clan, it behooves me to have the good manners to meet them with some grace and a recognition of *their* accomplishments.

I used to define the space designated in my mind as "home" by the name of my town, my telephone number, and my street address. But in recent years I have begun to feel that there are more important designators for me and that I need to learn them: the native trees, the native wildflowers—the first in spring, the last in autumn—wherever I walk. A constant flow

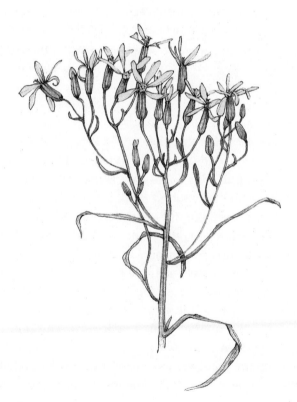

of questions results: I know that shrub growing along the path, and what its beneficial uses are, but not what spider festoons its branches. Nor the mushrooms that spring up unbidden in the grass. I *do* know what the name of the small, splayed-open ivory lilies nesting close to the ground in early spring is, and what bird carols me awake in the morning, but I don't know what the migration patterns are of the birds that match the seasons. *That* knowledge may be as or more important than my numerical existence.

I believe that knowledge of one's neighborhood, of the plants and animals and insects and rocks (and everybody else I've left out) that share our space, ought to be a part of everyone's lexicon of place. Surely it's not asking too much for each of us to know ten native plants, ten stars by name, ten six- and eight-legged crawlers and hoppers? But I recognize too that there are other ways of knowing home if you live in a city, a different awareness of place that brings its own kind of attachment. And if you don't know home, how can you care for where you live?

For me, accurate identification is an essential part of natural history writing. The words *natural history* on the cover of such a book imply a contract with readers that promises what they read therein is accurate to the best of the writer's ability. I happen to enjoy composing endnotes, not only because I have a pedantic turn of mind (I've been accused of being so pedantic that I italicize commas and periods), but also because I am a nonscientist. Endnotes say I did my homework. They may also introduce an interested reader to more information. I am grateful for all the marvelous, meticulous scientists who, over the years, have done the original research and written the superb monographs that provided me the information I needed, and recognizing them in endnotes is one way of saying thank you.

I feel the same about accuracy in fieldwork. Being *there,* cold, wet, tired, and hungry, provides a relationship with place available in no other way. And oh, by the way, it's also an effective literary device: readers who've had the same experience often react by identifying with and confirming your veracity or, if they haven't, being profoundly thankful that they don't have to sleep in the rain or be the recipient of a platoon of female mosquitoes' bloodthirsty attentions. Maybe they read on just because they're curious about what kind of a simpleminded stoic does put up with such discomfort, and actually enjoys it. Firsthand field notes bestow the particular freshness and sense of involvement that is one of the charms and strengths of natural history writing.

Observations written on the spot frequently contain errors of nomenclature or understanding, but those can and will (and must) be corrected in the quiet of library or workroom. Errors in field notes arise because of physical circumstances (taking notes in lurching, bouncing trucks is not for the uninitiated), time pressures, and ignorance, but they can be evaluated and corrected in posttrip serenity. This involves transcribing one's illegible, illiterate notes into usable English, a task only one up from scrubbing the bathroom floor.

If one simply piled field notes and research together, the result would be an unreadable gallimaufry. The writer's responsibility is to become a storyteller, to make research and field notes illuminate and enliven each other, creating a synthesis that is more than the mere sum of the parts. One needs to entice, captivate, and make all kinds of information—even dense and complex scientific data—so immediate and fascinating that readers are drawn into learning about this amazing and intricate world in spite of themselves.

Though one way to tell stories is to exaggerate and embroider facts, as Mark Twain did, within that fancy needlework abides a caveat: this technique is acceptable only when the reader is clearly aware that you are doing it. Most readers perceive that some facts are facts and some facts are fancies; a writer of natural history has a responsibility to make that distinction unmistakably clear. Another caveat: when first-person singular upstages nature, then the work slides from natural history into personal essay. In natural history, nature itself is forever front and center, not one's ego.

One of the ways I create order out of unrelated manuscripts is to spread them out on the floor. This morning glowing ribbons of color fall like fire opals across the row of typescripts. The windows in the cottage, other than the big square windows at the foot of the steps, are all the same size, vertical rectangles with three small square panes across the top; each of these latter has a wide beveled edge that splits the saffron shaft of morning sunshine into iridescent rainbows.

A very lethargic yellow jacket, moving as slowly as a first grader's finger tracing letters, edges across a rainbow that highlights the words *Pikes Peak*. Because I'm allergic to wasp stings, I'd ordinarily remove a yellow jacket as quickly as possible. But this one seems so unthreatening that I suffer it to remain. The essay on which the yellow jacket teeters is about the mountain that defines my horizon of home. I grew up in Indiana and remember it with full affection, but I couldn't live there now: it has no mountains. Or, as Frank Waters wrote, "by hook or crook, make sure you're born with a mountain in the front yard. It comes in mighty handy all the way around."

The big shallow circumflex of Pikes Peak's east face is the first thing I look for in the morning when I go out to pick up the newspapers, and often my last landscape view of the day. What I know of mountains and gods lies on that trusted horizon.

From fall through spring and into June of many years, the surface is edited with snow like scribbled proofreader marks. In the cold gray blue predawn light of winter, it is forbidding, bleak, remote. Some days clouds float above the peak like a *baldacchino,* sunlight streaming through as overly dramatic as the light in a Salvador Rosa painting. Some days the outline of the mountain retreats, attacked by ravenous cumulus clouds that nibble at its margin until they consume it, and some afternoons a lowering sun shatters on the profile in a blinding nimbus of light. Some mornings, when a white sky shutters the intervening mesas, believing in the mountain is an act of faith. But on mornings when the light is hard and the ridge line against the sky is as metallic and crisp as if cut with tin snips, a grandiose, grandiloquent mountain confronts the morning sun. And once or twice every spring, at dawn, while the mountain flank is still flushed bright pink, and the sky a cold, pale blue, the mountain balances a great, glowing white globe of a full moon on its northern shoulder.

On some summer days, clouds coalesce over the summit, clotting sky and mountain and foothills alike with a voluminous gray porridge. Afterward, the mountain reveals their baptism: following a July rain, the rock almost seems to steam when bright sunlight strikes the momentary glaze of graupel, the half hail, half snow that falls on high mountains in the summer. The storm grumbles on, leaving the foothills swaddled in a softness of light.

In the fall, of course, the rain becomes snow and then the peak reappears from the base upward with an operatic, curtain-raising sense of anticipation. The clouds lift, the mountain culminates in an incandescent white summit, accompanied by a fanfare of wind that braids a wispy snow banner off its crest. That must have been the way Lt. Zebulon Pike first saw Pikes Peak that November day in 1806, when he made an ultimately unsuccessful attempt to climb it. In 1818, Dr. Robinson, a member of Pike's party, drew a map on which he labeled the mountain, "Pike's mountain." That wasn't the only name the mountain ever had, but it's the one that stuck.

Two years later, Dr. Edwin James, a botanist with Maj. Stephen Harriman Long's Yellowstone Expedition, made the first ascent in mid-July; he observed the "deep red colour" of the rock we now know as Pikes Peak granite and noted its characteristic friability, "disintegrating rapidly under the operation of frost and other causes, crumbling into small masses of half an ounce weight or less," that persisted in "rolling from under our feet, and rendering the ascent extremely difficult," just as it does today.

The next recorded climbs came nearly forty years later in the summer of 1858; the second of these marked the first ascent by a woman. Julia Archibald Holmes, accompanied by her husband and a guide, reached the summit on August 5. She recorded her trip in a journal that she incorporated into letters to her parents. Her equipment list was astounding, including nineteen pounds of bread, one pound of hog meat and one of sugar, five quilts, topped off with a volume of Emerson's *Essays*. The next woman was Katherine Lee Bates, a Wellesley College English professor, who ascended by means of a mule-drawn wagon in 1893 and penned the most memorable and melodic image of all, of "beautiful for spacious skies" and "purple mountain majesties above the fruited plain."

Even here, in this gentle, wooded environment with its shrouded horizons, the shape of Pikes Peak remains in my mind, superimposed ghostlike on the webbed green landscape outside the window. I believe in learning about home, and the knowledge I gained writing this essay may be one reason why I carry the peak's familiar creased monolith on the horizon of my retina.

The yellow jacket has slowly trekked down to the middle of the page. It must find the cool inside temperature a little chilly for a six-legger used to being fueled by the heat of sunlight. Measuring its laborious movement reminds me that I'm goofing off. I recognize creative procrastination when I see it, for it's something at which I'm very good. Guilt helps one overcome plain procrastination, but creative procrastination is more insidious because it substitutes equally worthwhile activities that really need to be done for the activity you really *must* do and don't want to: I am the woman who cleans closets and neatens drawers, organizes recipes, and catches up on mending to avoid writing a first draft.

I did not come here to watch a yellow jacket, tiptoe behind wrens, calibrate greenness; in short, not to prowl the surrounding, attention-getting, bewitching world. Yet I can no more keep from looking out the window and assessing the branches and how they perform, checking a small body busying among the leaves, or wondering about a wasp's halting wanderlust on a winter morning than I can resist breathing.

I find something in these observations, in the questions they engender about who and what and why, in the quest for answers to when and where and how, and in the discoveries that arise from these searches, that stabilizes my life. If life is a search, then this is the path I follow: red cedar, Douglas fir, winter wren, rainbow spectrum, yellow jacket. And when there are no finite answers, there is at least hope and concinnity along the way.

Third Morning

My usual way of writing is to scribble, and cut-out, and write it again and again. The shorter and plainer the better. And read the Bible . . . if I feel my style wants chastening.

—Beatrix Potter

Which brings me to mushrooms, which Beatrix Potter, of *Peter Rabbit* fame, so loved and drew so beautifully. In these wet northwestern woods and meadows, when I walk up to replenish my wood supply, mushrooms are all over the place. What strikes me most is the overall difference from the mushrooms my daughter Sara and I collected at our mountain place last fall, a banner year for mushrooms in Colorado. At Constant Friendship we have several boletus species, mushrooms with firm fat caps and stems, and tube pores rather than gills, and many russulas that are so crisp and brittle that they literally shatter if dropped, caused by a microscopic variation in internal structure. These handsome russulas bear beautiful bright caps—scarlet, orange, golden yellow—protecting exquisitely precise fine cream or white gills.

This year was not only one of plenty in our mountains but one that produced species new to me, and I updated my old field guides with new notations of date and habitat with great relish. For the first time we found "lobster mushrooms," a jack-o'-lantern orange fungal parasite that infests both benign lactarius and deadly amanitas. Supposedly they are superb eating, but when the host has been reduced to dis-identity, my willingness to sample drops way below zero. They glowed a gorgeous, rich orange as if someone had dropped real orange peels on the gravelly slope. And beneath a small Douglas fir I found impossibly tiny white mushrooms that I'd never seen there before, caps smaller than a pencil eraser, on inch-high, threadlike stems.

Knowing the mushrooms of home alerts me to the mushrooms of Hedgebrook. Outside my door awaits a new set of colors and shapes, even of growth patterns, for the mushrooms are mostly new to me, and I can't wait to find out what they are. It seems to me that one of the things naturalists do best is to follow a never-ending path of curiosity, and a new bevy of mushrooms is made to order. Do they lurk in the meadow or mark a path or flourish under a tree, and if so, what kind of tree? Do they belong to a family group I already know? Who are their cousins and their uncles and their aunts? I prepare to set out on a lighthearted taxonomic pilgrimage; as one botanical essayist put it, "Plant taxonomists start out as shy persons who have simply put their lowered eyes to good advantage." I look forward to a pleasurable day of creative procrastination with lovely delicate spokes of gills, odd-shaped polypores, curves and flutes of caps, and clusters and drifts of fungi.

I drape my hand lens around my neck and dig out a couple of plastic bags (naturalists always have plastic bags) and a handful of paper towels and a pen to write a number on each towel before I bundle up the mushroom and record its matching number in my notebook. Before I sally out the door, I lay out sheets of paper in a quiet corner of the worktable to hold the mushroom caps that I trust will dutifully deliver spore prints by morning.

In the open grassy sward at my doorstep, a spattering of small mushrooms grow scattered across the grass in curves and arcs. Water-soaked, oyster white, the caps are all small-change size—dimes, nickels, and quarters. On mature specimens, the edges of the caps split slightly and splay up, disclosing wide-spaced gills that join neatly to the stem. The stems, even and smooth, have the same soapy feel and color as the caps, and are very tough as I discover when I try to detach one. Each stem holds a little knob of dirt at its base, collected on tiny fuzzy hairs just visible under my hand lens. I surmise them to be the common "fairy mushroom," *Marasmius oreades,* which often grows in rings, but final identification will have to wait for a spore print. If they are, they have a wonderful name, taken from the Greek: *Marasmius* means to shrivel, and *oreades* refers to mountain fairies. Folklore has it that the rings were supernatural places where fairies frolicked or dragons fumed fire.

Under a huge Douglas fir, the ground is ruddy brown with dead needles—a mature tree may carry sixty million needles; usually it drops its needles but not the twigs, thus building up this cushiony mound. This morning twigs do litter the ground, the orts of three back-to-back wind storms, a quick pruning at heights only Paul Bunyon could reach. Though the twigs I pick up are supple and pliant, the wind just twisted them right off the branches.

Sprouting out of this thick duff are a couple of dozen charming little mushrooms, neat and tidy bell-shaped caps precisely the same chestnut brown as the needles. Beneath the caps radiate a few, widely spaced, cream-colored gills. The stems are striking, as dark, shiny, and tough as sheathed electrical wires. Another *Marasmius* species, this one, *plicatulus,* generally grows under Douglas firs. In the Pacific Northwest, Douglas firs form mycorrhizal relationships with more than a thousand mushrooms, and establishing that association is necessary for their seedlings to survive. Most of the mushrooms I find today turn out to be associates of Douglas firs.

In the woods I spot a mushroom poised along the path. It resembles a hand-high, funky orange funnel with ragged edges, torn open along one side, and turns out to be an apricot jelly mushroom. They are so fragile that they can only be eaten when very young, and even then they melt when cooked, so most people eat them raw in a salad or pickled in vinegar.

Just down the path I recognize two saddle mushrooms. The first time I saw saddle mushrooms years ago, I had no idea that they were even mushrooms. *Saddle* is a perfect description, for they resemble miniature saddles (maybe even tricorn hats) perched on a grooved stem or, as one imaginative mycologist has it, a scrap of old dirty rag tossed on top of a stick. With neither gills nor pores, their spores dust the outer surface of the cap with a microscopic white powder. The black helvella is impossible to misidentify, with its distinctive charcoal gray color, and conspicuously grooved stalk. It's another Douglas fir associate, quite common in the Northwest. Its genus name, *Helvella*, refers to the Latin name for a small potherb; oddly, helvellic acid, which these mushrooms form with age, is poisonous, scarcely good "potherb" material in my book.

The day's treasure proves to be a diminutive white helvella. It has the generic fluted stalk and disheveled cap of the larger black ones, but is chalky white, almost translucent, ethereal. I wrap it most gently in an extra paper towel to protect it.

Scuffling along, head down, I boot aside dozens of water-soaked Douglas fir cones, the unmistakable cones that intrigue children because they look as if little brown mice scampered between the scales, back legs and tail trailing out behind. Playing cone soccer, I nearly miss three incredibly minute mushrooms that grow out of the end of one cone. They have stems no thicker than linen thread, caps less than an eighth inch topped with a minute umbel, off-white to palest mauve. I need my 20X hand lens to make out the cap's infinitesimal fluting. The mushroom has no common name, and its scientific one, *Strobilurus (Collybia) trullisatus*, is far bigger than the mushroom itself. When I try to remove a cap to get a spore print, it

clings so tenaciously that it won't come free; I'll take a mycologist's word that the spores are white, and assume that the mushroom's place of growth is diagnostic.

I continue, filling my plastic bag with single specimens, writing down where I found them, whether they're single or gregarious, and anything else I can think of that will help in identifying them. I've found over time that, in my general ignorance, I seldom hit the for-sure diagnostic characteristic. I try to make up for that by noting as many salient features as systematically as possible—cap size and color, gill color and characteristics, stem length and diameter, habitat—and, if there's time, doing a small sketch.

When I get back to the cottage, the first thing I do is detach the mushroom caps and place them on clean paper for spore prints, inking their number beside each so I don't mix them up, hoping that the color of the dropped spores will nail an identification. And then, for the few hours before dinnertime, I open field guides and, mushrooms in hand, enjoy cool stems and impeccable gills and evocative odors, lost in the pleasures of identification and description. When I get up to check the woodstove, I'm surprised to see it's dark outside.

And time for dinner. Outside, my flashlight picks up little white coins in the grass and I envision the multitudes of buttons underground, plumping up with moisture, ready to emerge in the morning, the incredible hidden vigor and vitality of this soil, this whole fertile, encompassing natural world that surrounds and reassures and invigorates me.

The next morning I sort through the debris of tentative identifications and check them against the color of the spore prints. A lovely clear, almost salmon-colored spore print belongs to *Entoloma nidorosum,* the livid entoloma. I found this mushroom beneath an evergreen huckleberry; supposedly when fresh, the mushrooms smell like bleach, but my nose can't discern it. I discover that entolomas are poisonous, common in the Northwest in fall and winter.

I pause to wonder who thinks up these awkward, outlandish names—"livid entoloma" indeed. Probably the work of some field guide editor. The trend to common names is such that scientists who author field guides are admonished that if a common name does not exist, they ought to make one up. Often the result is a straightforward translation of the Latin, usually unwieldy or awkward or both, like this one. I roll "en-to-ló-ma" around in my mouth like a hard candy, sucking on the syllables. Beats me why we don't learn the Latin names; granted, common names often have their own poetry, often pungently describe characteristics handy for identification, like "stinkhorn" and "saddle" and "death angel" mushrooms, but they are also imprecise since there may be a dozen species involved. So who cares? Mushroom hunters do—dining on a mistaken identity can result in anything from an irritated or upset stomach to an unhappy fatality that can really spoil your day.

A wood lover cap, *Naematoloma fasciculare* (*fasciculare* refers to the clustered growth habit) dropped a thick, velvety, purple-brown spore print. Wood lovers are charming mushrooms; these grew poised like small orange butterflies on the side of a tall stump. The stems are curved and twisted because they jam so tightly together, pushing to hold every cap properly upright to provide uninterrupted passage for ripened spores.

A cluster of small white mushrooms rooted in a big pad of very green moss are the last I identify. Between the main gills attached to the stem are inserted one or two shorter gills toward the outer edge. The spore print is white, showing up with a raking light like white baby powder on the white paper. White spores identify it as another common mushroom in these parts, the crowded white clitocybe, *Clitocybe dilatata*. I hold it in the palm of my hand and visualize the thousands of yards of white cottony mycelial strands weaving underground, masses and tangles and snarls of microscopic filaments from which this mushroom sprang. Beatrix Potter first proposed that fungal fruiting bodies—mushrooms—budded from an underground source, a contribution scorned by scientists of the British natural history community who refused to acknowledge that a woman who was a nonscientist to boot could make a valid scientific discovery. Her discovery went unacknowledged for years.

These fragile underground filaments swarming beneath the soil crosshatch it in a subterranean network like steel webbing in reinforced concrete, strands wadded together or spreading like tentacles, a vigorous, flourishing, thriving, ever-expanding population of connections, enduring from year to year, making a truth out of "forever." These unseen woofs and warps hold the world together, weaving a continuum ready to push, pop, or propel a mushroom button upward when temperature and moisture and moment are propitious. Mycelia are like the invisible threads that tie our lives together, ties with family, friends, community, place, country, and to other entities we don't even know about. We may not always know where we are in this complex unity, but we do know the strength of the connections; we're all part of holding the world together. I believe in mycelia.

Fourth Morning

I myself am convinced that there has never been a greater need than there is today for the reporter and interpreter of the natural world. Mankind has gone very far into an artificial world of his own creation. . . .

. . . I am convinced that we have been far too ready to assume that these people are indifferent to the world we know to be full of wonder. If they are indifferent it is only because they have not been properly introduced to it—and perhaps that is in some measure our fault. . . .

These are the people who want to know about the world that is our chosen one. If we have ever regarded our interest in natural history as an escape from the realities of our modern world, let us now reverse this attitude. For the mysteries of living things, and the birth and death of continents and seas, are among the great realities.

—Rachel Carson

In my lexicon, ten-thirty in the morning is a shamefully late hour to start work, but when it doesn't get light until almost nine o'clock, I tend to sleep late in the happy knowledge that since it's *not* light out, I don't have to be up at the early, early hour I rise at home, and I succumb to a gloriously sybaritic snuggle in warm flannel sheets for just a little more sleep in

41 ☞

the metaphor-for-a-cradle loft. I sleep soundly the whole night through, something I seldom do at the high altitude where I live. I ponder whether it's sea level altitude, the impeccable quiet (or if not that, the gentle soporific conversation of rain on the roof), the simple, sensible food, a comforting sense of accomplishment at the end of the day, a supportive community, some or all of the above, or some other mysterious and felicitous combination of circumstances that just *is,* and for which I am grateful.

In penance for such laziness, I clean up the kitchen. I tote the meager amount of vegetable peelings in the little canopic jar stored under the sink up to the compost can by the wood shed. I pick up another load of wood and kindling, and carry it back through the brisk rain that hyphenates the landscape with gray backslashes, computing the wind velocity. On the pathway I find a couple of nice rain-shined pebbles and drop them into my pocket. Habit.

Inside, on the corner of the roof under which the worktable sits, the steady raindrops play an erratic, irrational, now-and-then jazzy rhythm, not obtrusive but always present. The minute I record that, the cadence changes to a monotonous polka beat. The wind has died, and the cedars have transitioned from chorus girls twirling their sequined scarves to quiet branch tips, each holding a single, tiny crystal bead that spasmodically pops free and shimmers to the ground. It's a quintessential damp, dank, dark December day on Whidbey Island, very different from the sunny summery island I've known before.

To date I've known this island only in its halcyon summertime, when the bay sparkles and flowers bloom and birds sing everywhere, because Susan lives here and it's the time of year Herman generally flies us out to visit her. The insights these flights bring may be one of the greatest and most unanticipated treasures of my life, gifts from a husband who, by his own interests and skills as a pilot for over fifty-five years, has given me many trips to the moon on the sturdy gossamer wings of Icarus International Airlines (his wife and daughters' name for his plane). Flying between ten thousand and fifteen thousand feet enables me to view this country's magnificent landscape from the perfect altitude from which to understand it, low enough to see details but high enough to see connections, something impossible from the thirty-five thousand or more feet at which commercial planes fly.

Admittedly, I'm emotional about leaving terra firma any time. I feel too keenly the ties to earth slipping away as the plane leaves earth and enters sky like a great white pelican, wings spread, lifting gently up into its natural element. Bracketed between take-off and landing, I gain a view of earth spreading out beneath a smudged horizon, all the connected land forms rising and falling into each other, coherent, cohesive, comprehensive, beautiful.

Perhaps my shift in attitude also comes about because I momentarily leave behind some of my earthly inhibitions, my "nice girls don'ts," my curtsies to the queen. Without a cloak of comforting conventions, dependent upon two blurred propellers, life becomes infinitely more tenuous and therefore more precious. The things I care about I care about more, the landscape below that I know to be lumpy and bumpy flows into one heartbreakingly beautiful terrain, places where I have walked that now pass beneath the wing reach up and claim me. Most of my life I operate in a world of doing and working, and it may require this literal suspension in time and place to gain a new perspective on earth.

I scribble notes as we traverse the weathers going west, gathering on paper the transition from western mountains to Pacific sound. After we take off, patchy clouds cocoon us, one with an embedded squall that spits rain like black rice thrown at a witch's wedding, hitting the windows in a sharp staccato. After the squall, clouds float below like *îles flottant*, egg whites whipped into clouds and dropped by the spoonful.

The landscape in northern Utah amazingly resembles aeronautical charts, washed in subtle, airbrushed tans and siennas and umbers. Please *do* bury me on the lone prairie: ashes and bone are exactly the same colors as those that flow beneath the plane. Moiré patterns of ground, formed by variations of color that depend wholly upon contour, a little higher and drier here, a little lower and damper there, contours created by masses of water that poured out from glaciers ten thousand years ago: a landscape of what was. And in a nonhuman time span, what will be again. Were we to fly over this fifty million years hence, will all these memories be buried under tons of sediments? Will there be water sparkling around green hills? Or will there be vast plains of ice, throwing back cobalt blue glints?

As I always do, I search for the river so dear to my heart, the Green River that begins north in the Wind River Mountains in Wyoming, is deflected eastward by the Unita Mountains, then makes a sharp turn south through the east end of the range at the Gates of Lodore where we usually cross it. As we reach those familiar craggy red walls that mark the entrance to Lodore Canyon, named by one of John Wesley Powell's men on the first passage through it, an unexpected lump stoppers my throat, brought on by the powerful pull of a familiar and loved landscape re-experienced in the cool isolation of a plane's cabin. The swift surprise, the strength and pull of that reaction still in force after more than twenty years gives notice that the power of such places does not diminish.

Into the Great Basin, where valleys lie between mountain groups carved like chess pieces, the flat valleys are so clearly filled with thousands of cubic meters of debris sluiced off the mountains that one begins to have an inkling of what the gigantic fire hoses of melting glaciers achieved. Beneath the wing, farmland turns gray in cloud shadow, transformed into a pallid undulating sea with iceberg clouds, an Antarctic dream.

As we near the Cascade Mountains, a narrow, undecided ruching of clouds trims the horizon. Wispy clouds above diagram moisture and air currents, thin little clouds that burble the air flow over the wings, bouncing the plane. Ahead to the west, larger clouds, flat bottomed, take up battle formation, tethered together as if pushed from behind by a bargelike wind. When we reach them, I feel as if we are flying through a Tiepolo ceiling with its adorable clouds, designed for bare-bottomed nymphs and chubby putti to rest their little dimpled elbows upon as they gaze down on amorous mortals.

Soon Mount Rainier looms ahead, handsome and impressive in its stolid majesty, a huge presence cast in blue and white, like a beautiful Chinese porcelain piece. I wonder if the predilection for blue and white pottery in so many cultures comes from the presence of pristine white snow (or clouds) set off by ultramarine blue shadows (or skies). Our flight path takes us close enough to see the details of its bared ridges, the shapes of its snow banks, the essence of its power.

This morning, on this cool winter day in December, watching the branches of alien trees pattern their arcane dances, I remember that summer day and that magnificent flight across places that I knew well on the ground, and how they reached up across distance and time to implode my thoughts, impale my heart. Which says to me that knowing a place requires time, and that knowing is what leads to loving a place, that our concept of "home" is not just a human semantic fancy but a primary requirement of survival.

I believe that it takes time to develop the deep respect and understanding for the natural world that we humans must have to survive. Unfortunately, the contemplative character of natural history writing may not move mountains quickly enough; on the other hand, it may foster a longer-term devotion; things you learn quickly you also forget quickly. Nor does deep commitment come from understanding based on scientific data alone. Appreciation and knowledge of the natural world go together; love of a particular landscape is akin to love of home. But in order to build up a devotion to place, the acquaintance with one's particular corners of the natural world needs to begin early.

Without knowing or caring whose leaf turns red when, what spider casts that shining thread, what butterfly lays its eggs so its caterpillar awakens to a meal, being unaware of the great horned owl's call, or where the leopard frogs jump, whether bobcats prowl nearby, and what's around the bend of a river, we are left without understanding. We become trapped into seeing ourselves as dominant over a human-made world, not as a functioning part of a larger, natural, and harmonious whole. As middle daughter Jane says, "I also wish we had the imagination and generosity to just leave it be." The natural world needs our respect and solicitude: don't just send money, send love.

My generation has been accused of mucking up the environment, but it's also been pivotal in making massive changes in thinking and attitude and understanding, including many worthwhile and imaginative attempts to preserve and to educate. That has more often than not come about because we were raised by elders who took us by the hand into the magical natural world and instilled in us what Rachel Carson called "a sense of wonder."

Love comes from repeated exposure, the comfort of the expected, the knowing what's there so that you delight in the untoward—the surprising beetle, the unidentified plant, the quick new bird, the dazzling comet crossing the paths of familiar constellations with a different shape of light. Nothing can take the place of that trustful introduction in your parents' arms, or holding the hand of a trusted elder.

A young naturalist friend, Sarah Drummond, speaks of being carried as a child on her father's shoulders when they went for walks. When Sarah was three, her father, a fine lepidopterist and naturalist, pointed out different kinds of scat along the path, talked about what animals made them, what they had been eating, where they might have been going. Sarah loved sharing that time with her father: "When you see your parents so eager and animated about something, you know it must be worthwhile." Sarah's natural history expertise (and expert she is) came first from love and second from knowledge. She shares with her mother a passion for research and history. Sarah has received the American Museum of Natural History's Award for Young Naturalists the two years it's been offered.

Last fall, Sarah and I went mushroom collecting, just poking around, trusting in four eyes being better than two, checking out what's going on. Afterward, we sat on the deck, Sarah drawing while I tried to ferret out identifications. "Drawing helps me to know something for what it is, not just its name," said Sarah. I agree: I have long known that an excursion among the gills of a mushroom, a hike with pencil around the stamens of a lily, can tell me much and cheer me more. Sarah observed that we do the same things but in different sequence; we agreed that the back-and-forthness between writing and drawing is useful for us both. Yet it's writing with which I have cast my lot. I couldn't do both: art is too demanding a master. I am content to be an illustrator, not an artist. I draw to learn. It was never a conscious decision; over time it just worked out that way.

The cottage does not hold its heat this morning, I suppose because it's so damp. For this dry-country, sinus-desiccated Coloradoan, the northwestern rain is a phenomenon in itself. Dampness permeates my lungs, my eyelashes, my fingerprints, my thought processes. This morning I feel measurably weightier and slower moving, invaded by soggy spirits.

I drag myself up to feed the stove. The little monster *is* demanding. It doesn't request, it dictates that I go out and get wood to feed it. It has no respect for my work hours. It does not hesitate to interrupt me. It commands my notice like an insistent child. It uses congelation as a prod to keep stoking it if I want to keep warm. Its constant care and feeding would annoy me did I not reflect that friendship requires the same, plus a little more affection.

There have been moments when I've yearned for

a thermostat, but now I accept that the different rhythm the stove imposes upon my day has something of worth in it, something of connection (even if I didn't chop or stack the wood). Ironically, it also forces me to deal with that other life I thought I'd left outside Hedgebrook's gate: it reminds me that there may be no life that isn't predicated on interruption. I don't need to tell the stove what's for dinner, but I do need to fill its stomach and make my daily obeisance.

We get along, the stove and I. I keep the damper seven-eighths closed, tuck in a new log every hour or so, maintain the little round gauge on the stove pipe at one hundred fifty to two hundred degrees Fahrenheit. I do this not by reading the gauge but by listening to the small tea kettle on top—not hot enough to make the water burp and boil and use wood needlessly, but just hot enough to make it sigh with a contented simmer. I marvel at the way this little Finnish stove maintains just the right level of warmth for comfort. Keeping such a delicate balance is a small skill but, at the moment, one that I'm nicely pleased with.

The fire has gone down so far I can barely see any glowing coals. I slide in a couple of sticks of kindling, add a log, and leave the door open. When I return to working on the manuscript, I hear a "whoompf" as it flares up.

When I hunkered down to feed the stove, the pebbles I picked up earlier shifted in my pocket. Over the years, I've collected pebbles—ocean pebbles, river pebbles—by preference the size of quail eggs, choosing them for the purity of their curve, the precise rounding of their edge, their perfection of form rather than exotic color. A pebble is an obdurate personality upon which water has worked its will, turned it into an elegant oval that tells of places that changed my way of seeing and thinking, and taught me something of the truth of quartz, feldspar, and mica, of limestone and porphyry. Picking up pebbles rewards me with the psychological acquisitive pleasures of collecting as well as being distinctive reminders of place, better than a postcard, more revealing than an essay, more lasting than a trinket. Over a couple of decades, when I brought them home from wherever I'd been, I put them in miscellaneous small glass jars and bowls, always remembering to post a label in the bottom as to place and date. Since I've spent a lot of time on a lot of beaches in my chosen profession, I've gathered, garnered, and lugged a *lot* of pebbles.

Eventually, jars of pebbles proliferated onto almost every available horizontal space in my workroom. When my desktop was no longer visible, a kindly husband constructed two long, narrow shelves and mounted them high on the wall above the door and window lintels of my workroom. I arranged the containers up there where the colors shone through, where I knew the label on the bottom marked a memory of a place I'd learned to know through the feel and heft of its pebbles. I enjoyed seeing them arrayed on the shelves whenever I walked in. They were reminders of sequence, a token of how I'd spent my time as clearly as the spines of my books on the bookshelf did. They acknowledged a ceremony of living.

One evening I walked into my workroom and confronted disaster. The nine-foot shelf had given way, cannonading jars out into the room, spraying pebbles and glass shrapnel all the way to the doorway. Pebbles lay everywhere in inchoate heaps like spent grapeshot. I've never had a house rearranged by an earthquake, but at that moment I had an inkling of what it must feel like. My familiar workroom was a shambles, disarranged, out of context.

My pragmatic self got a dustpan, gloves to pick up splintered glass, an ugly orange bowl in which to toss the errant pebbles lurking beside a bookcase, beneath a chair, behind a door, in a shoe. Yes, the glass could be, and was, cleaned up. But the heaped-together pebbles had lost their provenance. I was left holding a handful of ragtag labels that had nothing to label. Which were the pebbles that belonged to "DESOLATION CANYON 1975 SUMMER"? How about "DECEPTION PASS 16 JULY 1992"? "BASE OF TONOPAH DUNES 8 MAR 1986 W/SARA"? "ALEXANDER SELKIRK'S BEACH, ISLA MAS À TIERRA, JUAN FERNÁNDEZ ISLANDS 11 JANUARY 1993"? "SEVIER DRY LAKE/TTW APRIL 1987"? "OLYMPUS (GREECE) WITH JANE 1981"? "SAN JUAN RIVER/HONAKER TRAIL JUNE 1985"? "RUBY BEACH OLYMPIC PENINSULA/SUSAN MAY 1991"? Reading labels brought back the ambiance of place, the time of day, the heat or the cool, but the small talismans they identified were disinherited, robbed of identity, disenfranchised, undifferentiated. The laws of gravity totally rearranged my point of view, exploded an orderly arrangement of time and place, assaulted memories, violated my sense of order.

Yes, the shelf got rebuilt. Yes, a few of the pebbles were so distinctive that I recognized what they were and where they came from and restored them to their proper labels. The pebbles again look lovely in other glass jars, noses pressed against their glass walls, as long as you don't know what they were before. It's just not the same. I'm adjusting to seeing them in their more prosaic setting, without their parentage of landscape. When I look up at the shelves, it's as if I had amnesia. It's the knowing that I miss.

Fifth Morning

In the end I want to be remembered as someone who loved well; this earth, all of its inhabitants, and this life. I want to have somehow made a difference to those whose lives I've touched and who have touched mine. I want to be remembered as someone with vision and compassion, humble and helpful. I want to be remembered not as the singer, but as the song.

—Beverly Graham

Outside the windows the branches are absolutely still, the light is fair, bright, no rain drums the roof. But the cottage is clammy.

I dress in cold clothes and climb down to start a fire. The cottage clock blinks. A power outage in the night must have discombobulated it. My beloved thirty-one-year-old self-winding watch has lost its get-up-and-go with age, and since I neglected the occasional winding that it needs, it stopped six hours ago. I honestly do not know the precise time, other than it's after sunrise and before noon because there's been no lunch knock on the door yet.

I've not listened to the radio while I've been here, not wishing its intrusion on my quiet, serene, balanced world. I twiddle the dial to find a news program, and am underwhelmed to learn that the NBA all-star game was canceled in Philadelphia, crime is down in Canadian cities but up 15 percent in the prairies. A new high for the NASDAQ. Words fail me. Maybe I should be thankful for slow news days. I hear the time and turn off the radio. I know all that's important for me to know today by looking out the window.

I already knew the date: December 7. On that Sunday morning in 1941, my mother was taking me to the ice rink to go figure skating when the news came over the car radio that Pearl Harbor had been attacked. Although it meant little to me at the time, it would come to loom heavy in my life. In those intense times, my love of country was shaped by an "honorable war" (oxymoron that that may be) that we fought because we felt then (and I still do) that civilization as we knew it was endangered, and compromise had achieved no solutions. It was a large event in my life, but it has nearly faded from view of anyone under sixty in our short life attention spans.

Where I sit this morning was under a thick ice sheet a scarce ten to twelve thousand years ago. Whidbey Island is a glacial moraine island, a heap of debris dumped as the last and fourth glacial retreat from Washington. The Puget Sound ice lobe nudged up against the Cascade Mountains to the east and dredged out the Strait of Juan de Fuca to the northwest in a cycle of glaciation and retreat.

El Niño and La Niña have visited us for centuries, yet we are just now discovering that they are part of the larger cycles about which we, with our short life spans, know very little. In an even larger rhythm, every fifty to a hundred million years or so, mass extinctions have occurred when huge numbers of species disappeared in a rapid, catastrophic stroke, changes used to define the main geological time periods, no Environmental Impact Statement required.

Global warming is writ large in landscape forms here. Doubtless, glaciers will be back. Our three-score-and-ten sound-bite vision lacks the geologic point of view.

This afternoon I have an appointment with Nancy Nordhoff, who envisioned Hedgebrook more than ten years ago. After doing philanthropic work in Seattle for twenty-five years, she wanted to do something more focused, wanted, in her words, "to give something back." She and cofounder Sheryl Feldman, a writer, decided to create this uncommon retreat for women writers. An experienced and energetic gardener, Nancy found this "generous, undulating land" on Whidbey Island and bought it in 1985. She refurbished the farmhouse, fed the gardens, restored the sheds, and oversaw the construction of six cottages that now house resident writers. Architect Chuck Dougherty, whose work shows the influence of the Amish with whom he had worked, designed cottages "peaked like hemlocks" so that one who lives in these cottages "lives within nature." Mike Page attended to the details of fine craftsmanship that characterize them. Here one realizes Virginia Woolf's criteria that "a woman must have money and a room of her own if she is to write . . ."

If I am any example of someone for whom this place works as Nancy conceived it, she has succeeded admirably. But I'm atypical; 90 percent of the writers come from urban situations, most from the West or East Coasts. Were I, like them, attuned to traffic sounds and sirens, I suspect I'd find this quiet rather unsettling, heating by woodstove a challenge, all this nature a little overwhelming. For one writer, it took courage just to go walk in the woods. One of the blessings of this place is that urban women can discover that they are surrounded by a benign and fascinating natural world that won't mug them. I doubt that there is any writer who has spent time here that isn't grateful for Nancy's "giving back."

As Nancy and I talk, it strikes me that both of us have strong convictions about contributing to the world in which we live. We both grew up watching our parents honor their own commitments to community (apparently, according to people I know who work on fund-raising with various volunteer organizations, if parents do not take on care of community, it's unlikely their children will either).

In Muncie, Indiana, where I grew up, when a member of the bar association died, all the lawyers gathered in the old courthouse to speak, Quaker fashion, about a confrère that they had just lost. When my father died, the words spoken and thoughts unspoken of his generosity and kindness, his skill and dedication to his profession, I still carry with me. They remembered that my father always had time to chat with young lawyers just getting started, and often tided over a few with a dinner or two in times when beginning lawyers were lucky to make three hundred dollars in their first year in practice. They spoke of what he gave back to his community in time and service. My father served demanding terms on the Muncie School Board for years, serving only if he was elected unanimously by the rest of the board; he always was. He made many other contributions, mostly anonymously; his example has been a powerful one for me.

As Nancy and I grew up, it became increasingly important to both of us to add to the world around us. For me, it's been the natural world and the organizations that care and protect it. I also appreciate the ways in which my horizons have been broadened in learning to care for what I love.

I came to my current relationship with the natural world purely by chance. I've told this story a thousand times in answer to the eternal question, How did you get started writing? I'd be happy if this were the last.

One spring day in the late 1960s, Nancy Wood, a friend and very good writer, called me up: "My agent, Marie, is visiting me and I'm running out of things to do, and I know she'd love to see your place in the mountains." Of course. Such things fit easily into a housewife's unscheduled life. "The place" was forty acres of graveled slopes, open conifer woods, tiny streams and a small pond and, most of all, an aspen grove in the montane zone at eight thousand three hundred feet in the Front Range, an hour northwest of Colorado Springs.

Marie rode to the mountains with Nancy and me, asking questions about the wildflowers along the way. After a hiatus of twenty years I had returned to artwork, a comfort when my parents were in dire health so far away in Indiana. I was learning wildflowers through a hand lens and by drawing them,

and the notebook filled with sketches was on the seat beside me. Sketching unknown flowers as accurately as possible was a mnemonic device I still use to cement details in memory—curl of petal, notch of leaf, intricacy of seed. When Marie asked about a particular flower, I referred her to that notebook. After several more questions, Marie asked out of the blue, "Why don't you write a book on Colorado ecology?" I chuckled. "Can I have the car, Mom?" and "What's for dinner?" were the meatiest questions I dealt with. I thought no more about Marie's remark.

When Nancy called to thank me for the day, she asked, "Do you know who *she* is?" in the tone one uses speaking to an obstinate child. Without waiting for an answer, she explained that Marie was one of the best agents in New York, that she specialized in nature writers, that she was Rachel Carson's friend and now her literary executor, and that she *never* took unsolicited manuscripts. Carson's *The Edge of the Sea* was (and is) my idea of the perfect book. But *me* write a book? Way too outrageous a thought.

Yet, like many outré thoughts, it insinuated itself in my head, and I realized that it was exactly what I'd like to do. I called Marie and asked for the particulars. She prescribed a *full* outline, plus three complete chapters. I bought a new packet of typewriter paper and a new typewriter ribbon—I've not felt so professional since! Naively, I typed three chapters, three to eight pages each, and a one-page outline, not knowing as I do now that I am genetically incapable of writing a complete outline. Grocery lists, yes; outlines, no.

I heard nothing. My resolve stiffened. I really *did* want to write a book about this marvelous place in the mountains this flatlander was just beginning to explore. Finally, a call from Marie: she'd been ill, she'd get back to me as soon as she got the manuscript from an editor she'd given it to, and she instructed that then I would need to write a *real* outline and *real* chapters of at least thirty pages each. That was late 1967; on Leap Year Day 1968, the telephone rang very early in the morning, New York being two hours ahead of Colorado. Marie had a rather high, quavery voice, and that morning it was higher and more quavery than usual. "My dear," she said, "Random House has taken your book." A stunned silence followed, during which I realized that she was aghast. She had an unknown client two thousand miles away and didn't even know if said client could write a coherent sentence; she later confessed that it was the drawings that had intrigued her rather than any text. And there I was, at age forty-three, writing about something I knew almost nothing about, unaware of how it might change my life. Now I know. The result, to the surprise of us both, was *Beyond the Aspen Grove,* a book about Constant Friendship, our beloved forty acres in the mountains, published in 1970.

Marie, who was also an uncommonly fine editor, gave me the chance to write a book and guided me through the process with wisdom and patience. By her encouragement and advice, she made possible the work that now defines my life. In passing on her dedication and love of the natural world, she gave me a gift that clearly lies far beyond a simple spoken thank you, which I can only repay by also passing on to others.

In my profession, the most telling example of "giving something back" is the work of Rachel Carson. She was a superb and successful natural history writer;

The Sea Around Us, published in 1951, was translated into thirty-eight languages, followed in 1955 by *The Edge of the Sea*, an exquisite lyrical exploration of the different kinds of seashores of the United States. When she was diagnosed with cancer, Carson used the precious creative time left to write *Silent Spring*. She sacrificed the peacefulness of her own life because

> the beauty of the living world I was trying to save has always been uppermost in my mind—that, and anger at the senseless brutish things that were being done. I have felt bound by a solemn obligation to do what I could—if I didn't at least try I could never again be happy in nature.

Rachel Carson's discovery and tenacious documentation of the perils of DDT earned her the vilification of chemical manufacturers and the slings and arrows of some members of the scientific and academic communities who should have known better (Beatrix Potter redux?).

When *Silent Spring* appeared in 1962, it changed the way we saw the world. Not only did Carson call for a halt to the use of DDT, but she called attention to the necessity of looking at the natural world as a whole, of understanding the interconnectedness of life, of acknowledging that what affects one organism will also affect untold others. She broadcast the tenets of an environmental ethic that became part of many of our lives.

In her characteristically modest way, she wrote to

a friend that she believed "I have at least helped a little."

We each give back according to our own concerns and interests, and for Nancy Nordhoff it was Hedgebrook. Nancy envisioned Hedgebrook as being "a place where women could be respected and connected to the land," and where professional women could receive and give support, where women could commit time and energy to the craft of writing. Writers make application by submitting a sample of their work and a statement of why they want to come; about a fifth of the applications are accepted. When admitted, writers receive room and board for anywhere from one week to two months, to become, as Nancy says, the "best possible writers they can be while they're here."

Here, in this hermetic solitude, without distraction, a writer must face *her* work and *her* self, no excuses of laundry to do or children to pick up or meetings to attend. The only interruption during the day (unless you wish it otherwise) is the tap-tap on the door at noon when one of the cooks brings lunch in a basket. (Shades of Sophie Hawthorne, who brought her husband's lunch on a tray, covered with a white linen napkin, and left it outside his door, lest she disturb him with a knock!) We are pampered by rotating cooks who create healthy dinners where even clearing your plate is frowned upon—a small detail to some, but not having to jump up and clear counts as a luxury for others like me. A small staff takes care of registration; three gardeners tend the lavish vegetable garden and fruit trees, everyone respects the sanctity of our solitude.

As a gardener, Nancy discovered early on that individual plants set their own directions, and it's folly to go against them. She realized that poor gardening is like poor writing. She prunes and pampers the gardens, watching life grow on life that has gone before, her gardening skills a metaphor for how she has developed this tranquil place. As we walk around the farmhouse, I'm amazed at what's in bloom in December: red and white fuschias; marguerites with tiny white petals and yellow button centers; pink yarrow and heather. A camellia bush, higher than my head, flourishes against the sun-warmed south wall, fat with buds ready to open in February. An ancient Chinese legend tells of two camellia trees, standing side by side, that marked the months; one grew a leaf each day as the moon waxed, its twin dropped a leaf each day as the moon waned.

I suppose one could make the case that what it takes to maintain this idyllic place of Hedgebrook might better be spent finding a cure for cancer or Alzheimer's: there are thousands of cuts and bruises in our world and not near enough bandages. On the other hand, it's the social and environmental consciousness of many writers and their powerful images and evocative vocabulary that call attention to disasters in the making or already upon us, probe means, suggest ways, and, by their literacy, identify methods of fixing what truly is broken, as Rachel Carson did.

I understand that it is we, the "haves," who have the affluence and the time to be concerned about the environment, who have the capacity to preserve, to ensure the continuance of the natural world that makes life possible, and *that* is an obligation that goes with the pure accident of being born in this country. Since we do not have to spend all our time surviving, we have a much different way of looking at wilderness. Because we enjoy a fairly benign wilderness (no twenty-foot anacondas, no poisonous frogs, no malarial mosquitoes), we take greater pleasure in being outside in a fascinating natural landscape than being in one where we are constantly in jeopardy. We have the leisure time to learn about where we are, to develop a sense of responsibility toward the land and, over time, a love of it. We have the opportunity to observe, to behave with respect, and to understand the penalties of misusing it if we wish to continue living on earth in good health and good conscience.

By pure accident of birth, I've had an extraordinarily privileged life. I was born in the United States of loving, caring, intelligent parents, grew up in a quiet place at a quiet time, watched people care for each other through the desperate Depression (when I learned early to "make it do or do without" and to wait to buy something until I'd saved up enough to pay for it), and endured a terrible war that deeply marked all our lives even though there were no battles fought on this continent. As an adult, I was blessed with a splendid education and a marvelous opportunity to do work I love. I've happily been cold, wet, tired, and hungry scribbling field notes that gave me valuable insights into a natural world that nourishes us all. I get to work in faraway places with strange-sounding names, to kick rocks and pick up pebbles, to indulge in my love of research, to look after the drawing of plants, to gratify my fascination in juggling words on paper. I write natural history because I can't imagine doing anything else with my life.

But that felicitous self-indulgence does not satisfy me. I would like to be a link in a mental food chain that provides reliable and intriguing information about the natural world and interprets scientific data for interested readers; I want to share my enchantment with the natural world and its intricate workings with anyone open to its wonders. Or maybe more important, to those who are not. For *not* knowing how the natural world works condemns us to misunderstanding it, creating untold disasters and a bleak future.

We need to know that spiders are *not* insects, and sea cucumbers are *not* vegetables, or what we do in ignorance will come back to haunt our children's children. Ignorance is no defense in the court of natural law.

Sixth Morning

The meaning of a word—to me—is not as exact as the meaning of a color. Colors and shapes make a more definite statement than words. . . . I found that I could say things with color and shapes that I couldn't say in any other way— things that I had no words for.

—Georgia O'Keeffe

This afternoon, as I near tomorrow's leaving, my mind chatter has already begun, that incessant sparking that accompanies getting organized. I note how acclimated I have become in a scant week to living in Oak Cottage. I know which way to turn the lock to unlatch the door (opposite from what one assumes), I've figured out the latches that pivot in a different way to open or close the windows. I know how long it takes to get the stove up to warming temperature. I know at which windows to stand or sit for the best light. Only today I discovered that there are shades in every window! I've been content without them, allowing the candlepower of the day and my own pineal gland to set my agenda.

The cottage has sustained me, conducive to long spates of handwriting and editing, and solidifying sentences on Susan's laptop. There's enough space, but not too much, so well insulated that I've never been cold despite it being December. I've relished comfortable and varied work spaces. The handsome cabinetwork and the care spent on detail has ordered my mind, day by day.

The knowledge that I'm leaving tomorrow and need to get organized prods me back into linear thinking. As I gather up, tidy up, the focus changes, the necessities impinge. I intend to send some things home in a box rather than carry them, which means I need to sort books, manuscript, pens, and papers. I pick up a handful of watercolor pens and realize that I've not done any drawing while I've been here, my accustomed way to establish the contours of place in my mind. The times in my life of blank page and pen or pencil in hand are pure serenity and enjoyment, of intense learning, and of occasional frustration until I prompt myself that I'm not beholden to creating a "work of art," only to preserving my own quixotic reading of time and place.

I walk downslope to the farmhouse; out of its front window sweeps a typical Puget Sound seascape that rolls across Deer Lagoon. Over the crizzled water rise the blueberry blue mountains on the mainland. This afternoon I bless my exemplary art history training, which gave me the visual world through the eyes of countless painters and sculptors whose vision was keener, more sophisticated, whose minds were wider than mine, who saw a world I never would have seen with my eyes alone, who ordered my way of looking and comprehending.

Once, as the soft colors of afternoon light change, an ethereal horizontal line of apricot edges the far mountains and fades to Naples yellow, and once a stripe of pure silver tinsel limns the far edge of pewter water, and I see colors through Vermeer's eyes; as the tide falls, edges of dry land emerge, enlarge, a fence appears, the proportions change, the syntax alters, I see the lines of a Rembrandt sepia ink sketch. No verbal description I could ever write will bring this segment of Puget Sound landscape back with such clarity.

When I teach natural history writing, I encourage students to do thumbnail sketches in the margin of their journals as a learning device, a memory sharpener. If you've once drawn a sprig of sagebrush, the turn of a daisy petal, you not only know that petal but have a sense of all petals. In following the nesting curve, the crisp or the languid edge, you commit to some special corner of mind a knowledge you did not have before, along with a growing perception of how a flower works.

I believe that drawing, the carefully observed tracking of form, is a necessity for learning. Nothing pretentious, only a simple recognition of Fibonacci truth in an unfurling bracken frond, a conch shell, a pinecone. Drawing is the nonverbal articulation of what one sees. And with practice and without knowing it, you are rewarded with a wonderful lagniappe: the connections between eye and shoulder and elbow and hand become more secure, and, simply by default, the drawings become visibly more skilled, your frustrations less, your pleasure more. I have little patience with anyone who wails, "But I can't draw!"

HEDGEBOOK · TIDE GOING OUT· DEER BAY 12·8·98

Inability does not come from lack of motor skill, but lack of looking and seeing and lack of patience. I know no one who expects to sit down at the piano and, first time out, play a Beethoven sonata. Drawing takes practice too.

As I finish the drawing of Puget Sound, I notice little wafty-winged things afloat in the air, almost colorless and indistinguishable from motes of dust that rise and fall slowly with seemingly little purpose, living through their moments on a December afternoon. Like them, I believe in living in the present tense.

When I return, I leaf through Oak Cottage's journal (each cottage has its own in which it is requested of every writer to add an entry). I did not write in it earlier because I had too much of my own thinking to do and didn't want to be ensnared by others' observations or awed by others' skills. I look at the unlined heavy cream paper with its deckle edges for a moment, intimidated by its authority and quality, and its lack of lines to write on. I take up the watercolor pens and, almost without thinking, limn the red cedar bole and branches that are framed in the kitchen window, overlaying different colors, hue on hue, scumbling a resonant patchwork of colors for which there are no names, like burnt orange purple and mauve green and emerald pink. In the doing I learn precisely how a cedar bole rounds, of the shadows that surround it, how furrows calligraph the bark, at what angles the branches grow, of what quality of green are the minute leaves. Shapes and colors, not words, tell how I feel about this quiet place sheltered by big trees.

Watercolor pens still in hand, I have a pang of recall: I can't help but think of my artist mother who saw that I always had art lessons and who made it possible for me to do what she never had the opportunity to do. Never able to go to college because she was responsible for her younger siblings, my mother painted china professionally in a time when that's what nice girls did. She brought me up on games, which I still think is a wonderful way to learn; she cherished words and we played anagrams long before Scrabble came along. She taught me to sew well and do needlework, which I've enjoyed ever since. She was one of the founding mothers of an art study group in Muncie that is still active. I've often wondered if growing up in more towns than she was years old because her father was a railroad president made her more dependent upon her own inner joys and satisfactions, which she passed on, subliminally, to me.

I seldom think of my mother without thinking of my sister Jane, the two of them inextricably bound in my memory. It's hard to write about my sister, because our difference in age causes so many blanks and because when I was growing up she was usually away at school. Fourteen years older than I, she died at twenty-eight of heart complications, the aftermath of a severe childhood illness, a talented and superb musician whose career was tragically broken. I learned the strength of women from her and my mother, who cared for her the last few years of her life, knowing she would not live, and still managed to guide an obstreperous teenager. I can still hear my sister's gorgeous soprano soaring in operatic arias whose words remain with me, and I still know the lyrics of all of Noel Coward's songs because she loved singing them. She discovered in graduate school, where she studied voice, that her real love was conducting, then considered the exclusive realm of men; she was only allowed to conduct practice sessions so was prevented from developing those skills further. Both my mother and my sister, because of the time and society in which they lived, never had the privileges that have come to me, and that many women today consider their birthright. That such talented, intelligent, dedicated artists were denied the opportunities that have fallen into my lap is an ongoing sadness, and an overwhelming, almost overpowering reminder to me to use my privileges well.

The only sound in the cottage is the soft crepitation of the fire.

In the midst of stacking manuscripts, laying sketch pads flat, I stop to gaze out the window, musing about other boxes full of papers, a memory that takes me to a splendid crystalline spring morning at Constant Friendship when I watched myself go out the door.

Standing on the steps that morning, I could see down to the lake, where tiny flashes of light sparkled along the shore, minute celebrations of being ice-free, the pond returning to its vivacious, bright self after six months of being icebound. On the far edge, the mallards that arrived a couple of weeks ago floated serenely. The mallards symbolized observing this place closely over nearly forty years: they arrived the second week in April and timed the season, something I would not have known had I not marked their arrival, year after year after year, in the log I keep.

I keep a log, or perhaps field notes (*journal* is too serious a word for what I do), to record the comings and goings of gray-headed juncos and humans, cheeky tassel-eared squirrels and skittish Steller's jays, ticks and temperatures, when the ice is off the lake, when the aspen turn, when the first pasqueflowers open. I've discovered that one's observational skills increase very quickly when one records carefully: the more you see, the more you see. Taking the time to record honors any relationship with the natural world and gives me the knowledge of what to look for when, the pleasure of anticipation. My tattings of words are simple baseline data that merely record a time that will never come again. How do you know where you're going if you don't know where you've been?

Journals or logs or field notes (like sketches) are seldom artistic masterpieces, but they are valuable and accurate accounts, written as they are, on the spot. No natural history writer should be without one. Nor, to my mind, should anyone who cherishes life on earth with all its intricate and unexpected convolutions, expected complications, its concomitant craziness. Even a simple list at the end of the day achieves usefulness when written over time.

The reason I stood at the top of the steps that morning was to open doors for John Sheridan, head of Tutt Library at Colorado College, where I have done the preponderance of research for my books. Tutt Library has open stacks, a fact only a researcher could love: often it is not the book whose call number I've written down that holds that lovely web of information or far-out fact that makes my job so fascinating, but the book to the left, or above or below, whose index reveals an entry that leads to a precise and happy and surprising addition to what I was originally looking for.

Two more storage boxes lurched up the steps

with John behind them. It's a mite unsettling to see boxes containing what I'd done for the past thirty years proceeding under an impulse other than mine, going where they would no longer enjoy the companionship of spiders and silverfish and camel crickets and widely fluctuating temperatures, but someplace terribly neat and tidy and air-conditioned. The motley crew of banker's and computer paper and miscellaneous cardboard boxes, each of which had several previous lives, continued to march by. At this moment they seemed impersonal cardboard constructions whose contents had nothing at all to do with me. Just paper, ink, defunct rubber bands, and spavined paper clips.

But of course they had everything to do with me, for those boxes contained all the manuscripts of books written and not written, essays published and unpublished, attending correspondence, reviews, the odds and ends, all the miscellany of a quarter century of writing. As I watched them go up the steps, I felt as if someone were removing my vital organs, one by one, shoving them in a van that would whisk them off to the mortuary.

The jumbled stacks of boxes ended up in a small, sequestered room at the library for cataloging. I began a preliminary culling, trying to make life simpler for a cataloger who, I soon realized, would turn out, by default, to be me. I am finding a surprising satisfaction in labeling and ordering a dismaying miscellany, installing all that stuff in neat gray archival boxes that line up with matching shadows on metal shelves.

The dismaying miscellany begins to take on a pleasing and surprisingly neat and tidy aspect. I vacillate between exhilaration that I have spent my time well, and despair that I have done so little. Cataloging has become a task I am anxious to have finished and a task I never want to end, and at this writing I have months to go before I weep.

I approached cataloging as a researcher, something I've been for the last thirty-odd years, a discipline that underlies the nature writer's craft. I'm astounded at the difference in volume between the amount of material associated with early, pre-computer books and handwritten note cards and the last. I was never that profligate with paper when I typed it myself (ten hours a day, ten days to type a manuscript that, try my best, was full of errors).

Joseph Wood Krutch opined that a writer writes because he wants to be read; perhaps such an obvious truth is only partially true for me—for me the journey, not the arrival, has enriched my life: learning, adventure, stretching the mind and the body, learning, the pleasurable company of good people, and more learning. Each box contains a segment of time and space where once upon a time I walked and wrote about, places I shared with family or friends, places I enjoyed in coveted solitude. Inside are cherished hours of wandering the aspen grove at Constant Friendship, tracking the insects on the new spring leaves, recording the new elk scrapings, writing about the alizarin leaves of fall on the wild roses, drawing the stiff heads of the black-eyed Susans, hearing the long-ago voices of three little girls now grown up and the now voice of a grandchild.

Inside the boxes lay the Dana Plateau and the summit of Mount Evans and gorgeous alpine fell-fields and meadows; dipping a paddle in the head-waters and sleeping on the endless cradling sandbars along the Green River; long days of backpacking in Grand Gulch and discovering the goldbug beetles; halcyon years of exploring the Cape Region of Baja California; canoeing the Assabet and Sudbury Rivers with a dear friend. Deposited in one box was a week alone in the Cabeza Prieta, sweating in a flimsy blind while I counted bighorn sheep. In another was the account of a first stunning view of Half Dome from Glacier Point in Yosemite. One box contained notes from sea kayaking in Magdalena Bay, and my first trip down the Grand Canyon with Jane a dozen-plus years before I undertook to write a book about it, and notes for a book Susan and I edited together. Thanks to the computer, it took vastly more boxes to hold a couple of dozen trips down the Colorado River in the Grand Canyon. Maybe best of all were those dozen or so eighty-mile trips I loved to row on the San Juan River from Sand Island to Clay Hills Crossing, flat water, bumpy water, gorgeous cliffs, wind, and big blue southwestern sky. There lay hours of sitting alone in Robinson Crusoe's cave on the Juan Fernandez Islands, gazing out over the Tasmanian Sea from the top of Kapiti Island, quiet days watching the Three Gorges go by on the Yangtze River, all the marvelous places that became home for a little while, because I am a naturalist and recording home is what I do.

But in another restful, thankful way, I acknowledge that these boxes, in the end, contain only the susurrations of a brief wind that once whispered through an aspen grove.

While I've ruminated about one kind of a closure far away in Colorado, here on Whidbey Island, I've managed to collect everything that needs to be boxed up on the table for another kind of closure. Manuscripts, sketch pads, pencils, hand lens, all the oddments of a nature writer's life. The watercolor pens lie scattered on the table, gray tubes capped or banded with the color of their pigment: dove gray, blue mist, olive green, Naples yellow, ultramarine blue, sky blue, saffron, apricot, lavender, their unintentional mixing a pleasure to the eye. Like beliefs, each of its own color, each of its own use, sometimes single but capable of being overlapped into richer meanings. The pens lie on the table as I dropped them, embodying no particular organization, united only by the mycelia of ideas. I tally their colors as beliefs as I pack them: ultramarine kindness, Naples yellow giving back and sharing forward, lavender respect, sky blue naming, dove gray learning, apricot accuracy, green friendship . . .

I close the box, miraculously having gotten everything in, and walk down to the farmhouse to pick up tape and an address label. I scuffle back to the cottage through bigleaf maple leaves the size of both my feet, admire a patch of gossiping cattails, contented with where I've wandered but curious about all the nooks and crannies of Hedgebrook I've missed. Here there were stones and woods I might have learned from, just as St. Bernard counseled in the twelfth century in a quote dear to my heart:

> Believe an expert: you will find something far greater in the woods than in books. Trees and stones will teach you that which you cannot learn from the masters.

These words (which open this book) are emblazoned on a door I made for Constant Friendship, one of my favorite avocations over the years being the embellishing of plain, ordinary doors. I jigsawed out two-inch-high letters, glued them on the door, and sprayed the whole door white, letting the serendipitous subtleties of shadow and light convey the message and remind me of what's real.

Bernard, a cleric who lived in France from 1091 to 1153, founded the famous Cistercian Abbey in Clairvaux. He lived in proverbially interesting times: he supported the Second Crusade and was involved in the theological confrontation with Peter Abelard. With age, he withdrew more and more into contemplation, recording his beliefs in a series of epistles. The many translations of Bernard's lines indicate their popularity over time; Shakespeare echoed them in *As You Like It:*

> And this our life, exempt from public haunt,
> Finds tongues in trees, books in the running brooks,
> Sermons in stones, and good in every thing.

Wordsworth followed in "The Tables Turned":

> One impulse from a vernal wood
> May teach you more of man,
> Of moral evil and of good,
> Than all the sages can.

Bernard's words continue to resonate in my life.

Last of all, I tuck a first draft of this manuscript into my day pack, ready to take with me in the morning.

Last Morning

*I must find a balance somewhere, or an alter-
nating . . . of the pendulum between solitude
and communion, between retreat and return. In
my periods of retreat, perhaps I can learn something to carry back into my worldly life. . . .*

*Actually these are among the most impor-
tant times in one's life—when one is alone.
Certain springs are tapped only when we are
alone. The artist knows he must be alone to create; the writer, to work out his thoughts; the musician, to compose; the saint, to pray. But women
need solitude in order to find again the true
essence of themselves: that firm strand which
will be the indispensable center of a whole web
of human relationships.*

—Anne Morrow Lindberg

Long before dawn I stand at the sink, drinking a cup
of hot tea, looking through the reflections into an
obsidian darkness, remembering what's out there
from six mornings' memories. I sense the reality of
what I know to be present but cannot see. The vitality of those huge trees outside, the growingness of
the grass, the beneficence of sky burst right through
the pane, like the meaning of a dream—a message
couched in other terms but still direct, unmistakable,
memorable.

Some fifteen years ago, I had one of those dreams,

the only dream in my life I've not forgotten. I don't remember exactly when it occurred, but I came across a talk given in the late '80s when I spoke of it being "several years ago." Because of its high mountain setting, the dream surely occurred after I worked on a book about alpine tundra. Perhaps I remember it because it gave me such an indelible, unmistakable message about my life that it comes back to me through the cold dark dawn of a northwestern December morning.

I was seated in a magnificent alpine meadow surrounded by a breathtaking glory of wildflowers, flowers flowers flowers as far as I could see—white and ultramarine blue, apricot and brilliant yellow. On my lap I had my familiar lined, three-hole pad of yellow paper, familiar pencil clipped to its edge. I could turn three hundred sixty degrees for a total view of this dazzlingly beautiful mountain world, animated with flickering grasses and flitting butterflies and darting insects, diverse lives intersecting in complex and elegant ways.

Idyllic. Idyllic except for one thing: I knew that there had been a nuclear explosion in which no one had been spared: family gone, friends gone, life as I knew it gone, no going back to the places I so loved. Dreamlike, I felt no devastation. I had survived for a little longer because I had been charged with recording how beautiful the world was, how intricately interwoven, and then, at some finite time of completion, I too would be released.

Until then, my task was clear: to get it all down

on paper, what it was like when bee flies arrowed between daisy centers, when the little apricot moths hid in the grass and fluttered out at my passage, when the mayflies rose and fell in diaphanous swarms and, if there was time, how the oceans rolled in and whispered out, how the rivers gathered and pranced downhill. My job was to pass on the fragrance of a wild rose on a summer afternoon and the sweet aroma of dried aspen leaves, the sinuous slink of a leech and the deft determination of a hunting wolf spider on the prowl or the stately grace of a tarantula, the eye-shattering light shooting off sun-glazed snow and the taste of fresh clean water, the healing sound of rain on dry soil, a pinecone gall's closely held secrets, a butterfly's pheromones loosed upon an unsuspecting breeze. Nor must I forget the falcon's stoop and the cliff swallow's swift death over the frothing rapids of a river. I ought to trace a harvester ant's journey and a darkling beetle's intent and a sleek weasel's wishes, and how they all interlocked in contrapuntal journeys, the comings and goings of each dependent upon the other, each part of the other, like the enfolding embrace of alga and fungus. I needed to make note of how a nettle stung and a cactus glochid embedded itself into your skin, how a palm frond rattled and an aspen sibilated. I was obligated to describe a Sally Lightfoot's swift skitter and a sea anemone's unfolding, a sand grain's sibilant journey from sand beach to sandstone to sand dune. So much, so much to get down.

I took up my pencil and began to write.

Ann Haymond Zwinger

A PORTRAIT

by Scott Slovic

Hers is a scholar's art. Strange to think of the process by which dust and sunlight and the spray of water from oceans and rivers work their way into printed letters in the naturalist's notebook, then into books, and ultimately into a library.

I sit on a chair in the corner of a small faculty workroom at Colorado College's Tutt Library, watching the author sort through her papers, her memories. The office symbolizes the process of moving from disarray to order, from the jumble of notes and materials on the desk to the neatly numbered gray archival boxes that take up shelf space on two entire walls of the room. This is, it seems, what the naturalist does, taking the mélange of perceptions that comprises experience out in the world, turning to the synthesizing realm of library research, coming back to the relative clutter of field notes, and then bearing down for the preparation of a manuscript. The irony of Ann Zwinger's current work in the Tutt Library is that this elegant, self-effacing woman, a scholar and artist who raised three daughters and then, in her mid-forties, launched a career devoted to exploring the vast and rugged world, is now tasked with collecting herself, the fruits of her work, for storage in a research library. This is hardly a job she looks forward to—this sorting of the self. I'm sure she would much rather be dropping through whitewater on the Green River, reveling in fear and exhilaration, taking mental notes about rock formations and animal life. Or sitting quietly, alone in the desert of Baja California, drawing heliotropes or describing the behavior of a nearby lizard. Anything but analyzing and ordering herself.

She pauses in the process of recording book reviews on a yellow notepad, to be transferred at home onto the computer disk that will later be used for her *Credo* manuscript, and hands over a folder that might be of some interest to me. These are Edwin Way Teale's notes about Ann, dating back to the late 1970s, when they were working together on the project that would become *A Conscious Stillness: Two Naturalists on Thoreau's Rivers,* a book about their travels together on the Sudbury and Assabet Rivers near Concord, Massachusetts, that she completed by herself after his death in 1980. Then she returns to her filing and annotating, a green-clad dynamo in the plain white-walled room, with shelf upon shelf of charcoal boxes. When I haltingly catch her attention to ask if she'd mind my using some of Teale's notes in her *Credo* portrait, she cringes—this is not what she wants, yet she knows it may happen. The naturalist becomes the object of inspection begrudgingly. But, then, this entire *Credo* has required a rare effort of introspection from her, replacing the preferred inspection of the outside world. "I'm going to turn my back and you do what you have to do." *But leave me out of this process,* she implies.

Edwin Way Teale and Ann Zwinger were a perfect intellectual match. As she herself suggests in her preface to *A Conscious Stillness,* the two of them shared remarkably similar habits of mind: not only their devotion to the nuances of the natural world, but their passion for the writing processes that lead to works of natural history. Ann marveled at Teale's fastidiousness as a writer: his awe-inspiring typing skills, his devotion to an objective, past-tense perspective, and his particular sensitivity to the process of revising rough drafts. She also observed that "Edwin was the quintessential note-taker" and used his journals to give his work "accuracy and freshness, and reading his notes, written in terse phrases, often in the present tense, gives one the pleasure of seeing his intelligent and receptive understanding of the natural world about him." Teale explained to Ann that he had learned the importance of note-taking from the great naturalist William Beebe, who had in turn learned this from Ernest Thompson Seton. Ann herself found validation for her writing process, and the passion for the world that leads to the writing, in Teale's obvious approval of her work. She also found validation of her struggles with the process: "He felt about writing first drafts as I do: I'd rather clean closets first."

Teale himself is widely recognized as one of the major figures of twentieth-century American natural history. He published more than thirty books during his career, winning both popular and critical acclaim. Like Ann, he was born in Indiana and served a term as president of the Thoreau Society. He received the Pulitzer Prize in 1966 for his book *Wandering Through Winter*. It was his habit to write a brief biographical sketch of most people he met, a kind of reflex of the natural historian. Composed in 1977, a meticulously typed page in the file Ann hands me reads "Ann Zwinger . . . Background Information." Teale's appraisal of Ann is telling. It describes Ann's family life, her education, her geographical history. And then Teale, the consummate describer of creatures, offers his concluding assessment:

> So capable, so poised, so self-assured, so able to express self, so [in] command of expression, so culture[d] and so wide in education and background, except for her warmth and human qualities, would seem overpowering . . .
>
> Wherever she goes, the world seems a little better—surrounded by a feeling of good will as with a shining cloud. Some of this inherited from her father . . . "a tiny man with great charm" Herman recalled. But all seems so sincere—and is. (As correspondent said about my book: "How much it helps to know you are on this earth.")

An addendum, handwritten by Teale, reads: "Never knew anyone with such wide-ranging interests as Ann."

I look up and Ann is immersed once again in her

sorting and organizing, dwarfed by the wall of boxes. Dreaming of her vigorous life in landscapes of searing heat, tingling smells, and eye-burning color, she toes the line and pulls everything into order in a windowless room of gray boxes and plain white walls.

One approaches the house at Constant Friendship almost without noticing it. The stained walls and shingled roof are mottled by sunlight and shadow. It could be an old barn, or a boulder with patches of reddish lichen. From the outside, it is unobtrusive, perched on a slope above a small lake.

It is April 10, 1999. Later in the day, we'll visit the Tutt Library at Colorado College, where Ann is in the midst of preparing her manuscripts for the special collection. This morning, though, we've decided to come to one of her favorite places in the world: her family's Rocky Mountain retreat. The wind is whipping, crisp—the bright, bright light hurts my eyes before we turn west into the mountains, keeping the sun at our backs.

My notes from the trip are splayed across page after page. How did I ever expect to make something from these pieces? Ann's running commentary during the drive up from Colorado Springs, cheerful and various, seems hardly coherent in retrospect: "We've shifted from sedimentary to Pikes Peak granite," she tells me. There my notes begin, a reference to our physical context, our movement through stone. "I love this view—all spread out. . . . Isn't that a knockout?"

Ann exclaims at the brilliant pink rock of Pikes Peak as we ascend to the higher elevations—it's a view she has enjoyed thousands of times, nearly every day since 1960 in fact, except when on the road. She tells me about her mother's frustrations: a talented artist who never went to college and instead stayed home to raise children and paint china. She tells me, too, how she loved her father: "a dear, marvelous man." She talks about her Swiss-German husband, Herman: "He's Felix and I'm a slob. We're the odd couple." She tells me her theory of perpetuation—how her mother reinforced her own interest in art.

"That field is full of mountains," my notes read. "Anomaly as east-west outliers, not north-south. Devil's Head. . . . We never would have built our mountain house knowing what we know now—all the gas we would use—thirty miles up, thirty back. It's the epitome of what we know we shouldn't be doing." And yet we continue our drive west, up into the sunny mountains. Ann tells me about the importance of sports for kids, about her own yoga classes. She is seventy-four years old—I recall a line from the chronology she faxed me recently: "Even though I was born in 1925 I am now officially forty-seven." I believe her, despite the bending of time.

We arrive at the gate to Constant Friendship as Dixieland is playing on Ann's favorite public radio station, and she's enthusiastically commenting on the music: "Dixieland! How can anyone not like Dixieland!" At the gate she promptly exclaims at the sight of the season's first wild candytuft. I've never heard of candytuft, it seems, and do not realize that this sighting constitutes one of the essential processes of Ann's life, the marking of comings and goings, the passage of seasons, the acknowledgment of natural phenomena. Only later do I recall the passage in *Beyond the Aspen Grove,* where Ann writes about these particular flowers: "The wild candytuft are so minute as to go unnoticed until they are in full bloom. I get stiff sitting on the cold ground, trying to get low enough to draw them. There is no solution; getting nose to nose with a one-inch plant is just simply difficult."

We pull up to the house a short distance beyond the gate, and Ann methodically parks the car, turning it around so that it's ready for our eventual departure. When we enter the house, the first thing she does is fill birdfeeders, explaining to me how the nearby trees act as protection for certain kinds of birds and recalling the efforts of squirrels to get at the feeders. The second thing is to make notes in her blue, three-ring binder about the candytuft, about the lake being open, ice free. "Things are really late this year," she comments. Recording observations in her notebook and chatting with me at the same time, Ann jokes that the downy woodpecker we can see through the window looks like a used car salesman.

Ann and Herman bought their forty mountain acres north of Woodland Park in 1963. Although they have a beautiful old stucco house in Colorado Springs, not far from the campus of Colorado College, this mountain place is truly the heart's home. The whole story of their arrival at what they came to call "Constant Friendship" is told in Ann's first book, *Beyond the Aspen Grove*, published in 1970. From the outset she notes the irony of claiming to "own" this land:

> It has since turned out to be precisely the other way around. It is we who belong to the land. Beginning to know these mountain acres has been to discover a puzzle with a million pieces already set out on a table. Occasionally a few pieces fit together and we gain another awareness of the land's total pattern of existence, of its intricate interdependencies, enhanced by knowing that the puzzle will never be completed.

It's clear from Ann's enthusiasm today, thirty-six years after her arrival at this place, that the delightful puzzle of its existence is far from complete. There is a vigorous freshness to her movements. The rituals of arrival and caretaking show no weariness or loss of interest. After filling the birdfeeders and recording the first observations in the logbook, Ann begins an extended regimen of watering potted plants throughout the house. When Ann was working on *Beyond the Aspen Grove*, she and her family stayed without plumbing and electricity in a simple mountain cabin, constructed by hand in 1967–68, that still stands on the land. This new house was built in 1975. Although only thirty-two by thirty-two feet, the building has a spacious feel to it, with a large, high-ceilinged family room and library attached to a dining area and kitchen, leading out to a porch clearly designed for family gatherings and parties, overlooking the glistening pond. A second, smaller porch, also facing out toward the water, is where the birdfeeders are located. A bedroom is tucked away on the ground level; a shared workroom is up above, beyond spiraling stairs, with windows on all four sides and a bookcase loaded with field guides. Ann tells me that she asked architect Clifford Nakata to design the house "like a snail shell." It has many places to sit, listen, and take in sunlight and colors. I have the sense of both deliberateness and randomness. From where I sit in the open living room and kitchen/dining complex, I count seven windows, with light of different intensity entering through each. On this brilliant morning there are sprinkles and sprays of light on the surface of the wind-dappled lake, reflected on the ceiling so that the house takes on the same shimmer and movement.

I muse about the chapter called "The Lake" in *Beyond the Aspen Grove,* with its faint and ironic echoes of Henry David Thoreau's *Walden.* "This lake," she writes, "is the eye of the land." I hear Thoreau in Ann's words. "The land's changes," she continues, "are seasonal, expected; the lake's are swift, expressive, momentary, subtle. The lake changes from rain-dimpled to sparkling blue to flat brown within the hour, from misty sheen to bottomless black within the day. Looking down from my ridge above the lake,

I see the water, dark, clear, and deep. Sitting among the sedges at the edge, the surface gleams wide, flat, and opaque." Like Thoreau, Ann displays the naturalist's fascination with patterns and anomalies. Much of *Walden* revels in the changeability of the famous New England pond, just as "The Lake" savors the mercurial shifts of this small body of water in the Rockies. Whereas Thoreau made a point of noting the extreme depth of Walden Pond (102 feet at its deepest point) and clearly sought to use the depth of water as an analogy for the hoped-for depth of his prose, Ann writes, with some self-deprecation, "The deepest part of the lake is about twelve feet and lies off center, toward the dam." What this prose lacks in metaphysical profundity, though, it compensates for with painterly flair and observational detail.

For half an hour Ann disappears; I hear clanking buckets and water running from the kitchen faucet. She leaves me to experience the place, to look around. The walls are full of artwork, ranging from Herman's aerial photographs to their daughters' paintings and drawings; I recall the evening before, in the family room back in Colorado Springs, as Ann and Herman walked me through a loving tour of the many works of art produced years ago by Susan, Jane, and Sara. Occasionally I catch glimpses of Ann going about her business, dressed in a teal green sweater and corduroys with a white turtleneck. No wonder she chose to wear her Nike running shoes this morning. She is a vision of energy and order, moving through this process of caretaking. I hear water running, dry flowers being plucked and pruned. Ann talks to the plants as she works.

I find myself thinking about the name of this mountain home, "Constant Friendship." I first visited here three years ago, when Ann received the Orion Society's John Hay Award for distinguished lifetime achievement as a nature writer. There were about twenty of us who came together that weekend to celebrate Ann's work, not including Herman and daughters Jane and Sara. Back home in my office I have a photograph, taken by Herman, of most of the celebrants on the large porch at Constant Friendship—it was a sunny spring morning, much like this one. In the picture, I recognize old friends of Ann's and many close colleagues, such as Gary Paul Nabhan, Robert Michael Pyle, and Pattiann Rogers. I see several of the young writers who think of Ann as an informal mentor: Sarah Rabkin, Pat Musick, and Jan DeBlieu. One of her great contributions to the field of natural history writing, I realize, is not only how the model of her life and work has inspired generations of younger women nature writers, but the generous guidance and encouragement she has offered to up-and-coming writers, some of whom, such as Terry Tempest Williams, have become major artists themselves. There are also editors and scholars, such as Chip Blake and SueEllen Campbell, in this photograph. Friendship, Ann Zwinger style, is all-inclusive and welcoming. I fondly remember the extraordinary warmth of that occasion. At one point, after lunch, Ann slipped away from her duties in the kitchen and

joined me out on the front stoop. She and I had cor-
responded for several years, ever since I had invited
her to serve on the advisory board for the Association
for the Study of Literature and Environment in 1992,
yet we had never had an opportunity to sit quietly
and talk. "I've been wanting to tell you," she began,
"how much I appreciate your contribution to this
field through ASLE and your writing. You bring so
much to these gatherings." I remember thinking,
"What a generous soul, what a kind and gracious per-
son." In the group photograph, Ann, the focus of the
party, is standing in the back row, to the side, mostly
in shadow. Having brought these friends together,
she steps back and observes. The smile on her face is
calm and genuine.

Constant Friendship, Constant Friendship. Apart
from the drama of her adventures, the unforced elegance of her prose, and the painterly brilliance of
her natural descriptions, Ann Zwinger is known in
the community of nature writers and ecocritics as
a constant and reliable and gracious friend. The
name of the mountain home itself is an inherited
one. She tells the story in *Beyond the Aspen Grove* of
how her daughter Susan, then in high school, had
just completed an English assignment on her family
history when they bought the mountain property
and had learned that her great-great-great-great-
great-grandfather John Haymond, after his arrival
in America from England in the 1730s, had named his
homestead Constant Friendship. This name, adopted
as a family legacy, takes on new meaning—real

meaning—in the context of the Zwinger family's engagement with the mountain place and generous relationships with so many human friends.

Like her children, Ann has an abiding interest in family history, a strong sense of where she comes from. In offering a chronology of her life, she notes John Haymond's immigration to this continent in 1734, where he took up work as a carpenter. Her father, William Thomas Haymond, was born in Cowan, Indiana, in 1880. He attended Indiana University Law School and then settled in Muncie. Helen Louise Glass, Ann's mother, was born in Huntington, Indiana, in the mid-1880s, the descendant of German immigrants. Ann's sister Jane was born in 1910 and later attended the University of Michigan and the Cincinnati Conservatory of Music, where she embarked on a successful singing career; poor health forced her to give up school, and she died in 1938 from the results of misdiagnosed rheumatic fever during World War I.

Ann Haymond was born in Muncie in 1925, following her mother's difficult pregnancy. She recalls her father as a respected and well-loved member of the community, and attributes much of her own industriousness and love of nature to him. Her mother was, in a sense, a frustrated artist, whose family obligations restricted her to painting china; she passed along her love of the arts to her daughters. Ann also carries with her a fierce professional dedication, a desire to do her own creative and scholarly work in addition to being a proud and devoted wife and mother. Some of this drive must come from her memory of her mother's thwarted artistic talent.

Ann attended Burris High School in Muncie, the "laboratory school" for Ball State University, then known as Ball State Teacher's College. She entered Wellesley College in 1942, graduating four years later with honors and a degree in art history. After graduation, Ann promptly began an M.A. program in art history at Indiana University, having received a teaching assistantship. Married briefly while in Bloomington, she became a mother in 1947, with the birth of Susan. Juggling various responsibilities, Ann continued to work on her M.A., including a thesis on Louis Sullivan and Walt Whitman, completing her degree in 1950. In the fall, Ann and Susan moved to Massachusetts, where Ann took on a sabbatical replacement position in art history at Smith College. Her academic career path seemed clear.

In 1951, while teaching at Smith, Ann met Captain Herman H. Zwinger, a pilot in the United States Air Force, and they enjoyed a whirlwind courtship for two weeks before Herman was sent to Saudi Arabia for a year with the Air Rescue Service. Ann stayed behind, beginning her doctoral work in art history at Radcliffe College and conducting research in the Fogg Museum at Harvard. Herman returned and married Ann in 1952, and they moved with Susan to his next post in West Palm Beach, Florida. Ann had completed her residence requirements for the doctorate but had no opportunities to continue her research. She did lead art history discussion groups for the American Association of University Women (AAUW) in Florida. The responsibilities of motherhood continued to mount as well, with the birth of Jane in 1954 and Sara in 1956. Ann recalls lying on her back in West Palm Beach, pregnant with Sara, with Rachel Carson's newly published *The Edge of the Sea* propped on her belly.

Herman was posted to Arkansas in 1956, and then to Kansas City in 1958. His family followed. In Arkansas, they lived on a farm three miles from the small town of Pocohontas. Ann taught adult education courses at the University of Kansas City from 1958 to 1960. Herman spent 1959 as commander of a radar site at Miyako Jima. Then, in 1960, he received his final post at NORAD in Colorado Springs. Ann continued to volunteer with the local Girl Scouts, as she'd done in Arkansas. She also taught art for a few years at nearby Benet Hill Academy. In 1965, Herman retired from the Air Force and Susan left home to attend Cornell College in Iowa. That year the family began one of its most important rituals: Thanksgiving dinner with the turkey cooked in the cabin's woodstove at Constant Friendship. The dining area at the mountain home is decorated today with family photographs taken year after year on Thanksgiving.

A major new phase in Ann's life began in 1967 when her friend Nancy Wood, a fiction writer and poet, introduced her to New York literary agent Marie Rodell. Ann has told this momentous story several times in her books, and does so again in her *Credo* essay. At the age of forty-two, she began her life as a natural history writer. At the same time, Herman, an extremely skilled pilot who had been flying for nearly three decades in the Air Force, purchased his first airplane; in 1969, he replaced his first plane with a Beech Baron 8008R, which the family named "Icarus International Airlines." In her books, Ann often refers to the bird's-eye view of the land she has enjoyed over the years from Herman's plane.

While working on this portrait, one of the things I most wanted to know was how Herman has reacted to Ann's busy career, especially when she was just starting out. In a good-humored letter, he explains:

> When Ann began to write somewhere around 1969 or 1970, I really didn't believe it would be an all-consuming ambition. Wrong. She slowly developed an ethic of working and writing that overshadowed everything else. How did this affect me? Well, I am a totally self-sufficient individual; I can fix just about anything that needs repair, I love to cook, and I have a variety of interests to occupy the mind.

In the beginning, Ann herself was not quite sure what she'd gotten herself into by accepting Marie Rodell's invitation to prepare a manuscript on Colorado ecology: "I just kind of mucked along," she told me when I visited her in Colorado Springs in April of 1999. Herman recalls that as an Air Force officer, he took the phrase "Duty, Honor, Country" very seriously and had, in fact, accepted hardship posts that included a year in Saudi Arabia and a year on a remote island off the coast of China during the early years of the marriage. Ann, he explains, "is equally devoted and duty bound to her career as a writer, and I respect that, however difficult it is sometimes for me when I want to ask her something or communicate with her. Once she gets wrapped up in thought, I'm outta there." Difficulties and frustrations aside, his pride in Ann's literary achievement and respect for her professional devotion are clearly evident.

Beyond the Aspen Grove appeared in 1970. This might have been both the beginning and the end of Ann's writing career, but in the process of having the technical aspects of her first book checked by professional scientists, she was befriended by Beatrice Willard, president of the Thorne Ecological Institute in Boulder and a former professor and director of the Department of Environmental Sciences at the Colorado School of Mines. Willard later recalled that she had immediately "recognized [Ann's] exceptional talent for conveying scientific facts to lay people in vivid terms and a most delightful manner—both by words and by delicate, accurate drawings. We agreed that we would work together on a book on alpine tundra, an undertaking we both viewed with enthusiasm." After three years of research and writing, *Land Above the Trees: A Guide to American Alpine Tundra* was published in 1972. The book explains the primary physical features and processes of "the alpine world," surveys major alpine regions in the United States, and concludes with a conservationist reflection, focusing on the jeopardy of alpine landscapes. "Until recently," the book notes, "no one ever thought of wilderness as an irreplaceable, exhaustible resource. Now we know that the wilderness can be exhausted, and this is most poignantly true of the alpine tundra."

Seldom, in her many books, does Ann's writing approach even this degree of political aggressiveness. Normally, her goal is to sweep up her readers, whether nature enthusiasts or not, in her own sense of wonder and excitement. On February 15, 1988, she joined Edward Lueders and Gary Paul Nabhan for a public dialogue at the University of Utah, the transcript of which was later published in *Writing Natural History: Dialogues with Authors*. "I have a friend," Ann noted, "whose idea of roughing it is when the color television is out at the Hyatt—and *that's* my audience. If I can say to somebody like that, 'There's something real and vital and exciting out there,' catch their attention, pique their interest, nudge their curiosity, that's the audience I want to reach." To reach such readers, she suggests, requires subtlety and the expression of joy and curiosity rather than angry browbeating.

Peter Wild begins his biography of Ann for Scribner's *American Nature Writers* with an animated description of her running the rapids on the Green River, taken from the book, *Run, River, Run,* the work published in 1975 that officially placed her in the ranks of the country's most distinguished natural history writers, earning her the John Burroughs Medal in 1976. It was at the Burroughs ceremony that she met Edwin Way Teale for the first time. This is indeed one side of Ann's work and personality: the barely controlled joy of experience; the willingness to take personal risks, whether by whitewater or simple desert isolation; and the ability to notice the world, to pay attention, even while racing through it with a paddle in her hands and her heart in her throat. In this book, Ann's writing hit full stride, showing a combination of adventure narrative and descriptive elegance woven together with intricate natural history detail, backed up with thirty pages of technical citations. By this time, her family had also come to accept her work, and Ann realized the importance of her professional life as a model for her daughters: "If mom can do it, anyone can do it," she hoped her girls would think. Indeed, Susan had by this time completed an M.F.A. in writing from the University of Iowa and was enrolled as a doctoral student at Penn State in art, psychology, and education. Jane had graduated from the Kansas City Art Institute. And Sara was an undergraduate at Willamette University in Oregon, with a double major in environmental science and urban/regional government. Today, thinking about her role as a mother, Ann states, "perhaps my greatest privilege is three daughters who are so different and with whom I have the most precious, warm, delightful, devoted relationships in my life." Another joyful relationship began in 1990, when granddaughter Sally Ann Roberts, named after her mother and grandmother, was born to Sara.

By the mid-1970s, honors began piling up. In

addition to the Burroughs Medal, Ann received an honorary doctorate from Colorado College in 1976. A year later, the Garden Club of America awarded her its Sarah Chapman Francis Medal and Wellesley College acknowledged three distinguished nature writers at once (Sally Carrighar, Marjorie Stoneman Douglas, and Ann) with the Alumnae Achievement Award. Despite and because of her busy writing life, Ann continued her life of public service, joining the board of American Electric Power in 1977, being elected president of the Thoreau Society in 1982 and joining the John Burroughs Association board in the same year, and accepting a second term as Thoreau Society president in 1983. She now serves on the board of PBS Channel Six in Denver.

The books, too, continued to appear. *Wind in the Rock* was published in 1978, followed by *A Conscious Stillness* in 1982. In 1970, the family had begun visiting Baja California. Her first book about this region, *A Desert Country Near the Sea,* came out in 1983. This is the year, too, when she began routinely doing public talks and readings and teaching stints at Colorado College and various other institutions around the country. Many of her occasional articles and lectures were later published in *The Nearsighted Naturalist* in 1998. She began working on *The Mysterious Lands,* her ambitious examination of the four desert regions of the American Southwest, in 1985—the book was completed and published four years later. In 1986, two more Baja-related volumes were published: edited collections of naturalist John Xántus's letters.

Colorado II was published in 1987, followed by *Utah II* in 1990. *Aspen: Blazon of the West,* with photographs by Barbara Sparks, was printed in 1991; that year Ann held an endowed chair at the Hulbert Center for Southwest Studies at Colorado College and also received the Distinguished Achievement Award from the Western Literature Association.

In 1992, Ann and her daughter Susan, an up-and-coming nature writer, had a mother-daughter dialogue during a plenary session at the Western Literature Association Conference in Reno. Susan's first book, *Stalking the Ice Dragon: An Alaskan Journey,* had appeared a year earlier, dedicated to "my three favorite nature writers: Rachel Carson, who started us thinking; Ann Zwinger, who raised me to think; and Ed Abbey, out there in his desert." It was obvious from the conversation that Ann and Susan share a love of art and wild places and natural-history knowledge and enjoy each other's company. Equally striking, though, were their very different attitudes toward environmental activism, Ann being the more restrained and cautious conservationist, while Susan is inclined toward outspoken response. In *Still Wild, Always Wild,* a book for the Sierra Club about the Mojave Desert, Susan yoked together her literary skill and her concern for environmental protection. Ann and Susan coedited *Women in Wilderness* in 1995, a year after Ann's *Writing the Western Landscape: Mary Austin and John Muir* appeared. Susan published another major book of adventure, natural history, and politics—*The Last Wild Edge: One Woman's Journey from the Arctic*

Circle to the Olympic Rain Forest—in 1999. In her introductory note to Ann's essay for the *Women in Wilderness* collection, Susan remembers, "As I was growing up, I knew her only as a full-time mother. For years her creativity found outlet . . . in volunteer work, cooking, and sewing most of our clothes." Later, "about the time most mothers are suffering empty-nest syndrome, she was drawing nests, studying the birds that lived in them, and capturing the insects on which they dined." When it's her turn to comment on Susan for the same volume, Ann observes, "I inherited my wilderness genes from my daughter. . . . Susan brought me up from a very timorous housewife to a rabid seeker of solitude."

Twenty years after the publication of *Run, River, Run,* Ann published another important study of a famous western river, *Downcanyon: A Naturalist Explores the Colorado River through the Grand Canyon.* This book shared the Western States Book Award for Creative Nonfiction in 1995. In this book, the author's background in the visual arts comes through not only in the pen-and-ink sketches, but in extravagantly beautiful word-painting:

> Cauliflowers of turquoise fume into the putty-colored Colorado, cusps of bright blue Havasu Creek water marbling the tan river and swirling back upstream—Havasu Creek, at Mile 156.7, is second only to the Little Colorado in the amount of water it carries to the river. It is also derisively called "Have-a-Zoo," for the numbers of people that crowd its pools in the summer time. And with good reason—water of a

divine temperature fills the travertine-formed pools, which have every depth and water flow necessary to entice bathers of every age and persuasion.

My first time at Havasu Island I relished sitting right at the edge of the creek where the water's rushing constantly rearranged and moved the green out of its way. Slender green grasses, horsetails and rushes, and trees with fluttering thin leaves were arrayed with a greenery so variegated that this small niche looked designed and planted, tended and mani-cured, by a master gardener bent on creating a pocket park with every shade and shape of green possible.

Image, information, social commentary, story. These elements stream together like the currents of the Colorado, minor flows within the larger narrative, which begins upstream at Lees Ferry and works its way, at book's end, to Mile 278.5, at the Grand Wash Fault. This work demonstrates Ann Zwinger at the peak of her art, joking and exclaiming, noticing and explaining.

Yosemite: Valley of Thunder appeared in 1996, and more books are sure to come. Ann's travels in recent years, to Egypt and New Zealand, to the Queen Charlotte Islands with Susan and to Dordogne with Sara, seem likely to have produced piles of notes, raw ciphers that may work their way into essays ("maybe," she says). In 1999, Ann journeyed to Antarctica for the first time. "There is more day to dawn," Thoreau wrote at the end of *Walden*. "The sun is but a morning star." At age seventy-four, one of the elders of her chosen discipline, Ann has no plans to be "sitting on the front porch in a rocking chair" anytime soon.

I find myself thinking of the passage in Ann's *Credo* where she describes her habit of decorating doors at the mountain house:

> One of my avocations over the years has been embellishing doors. One I made bears the excerpt from one of St. Bernard's epistles that opens this book ["Believe an expert: you will find something far greater in the woods than in books. Trees and stones will teach you that which you cannot learn from the masters"]. I cut out two-inch high letters with a jigsaw, glued them on the door, and sprayed the whole door white, allowing the serendipitous subtleties of shadow and light to convey a message that spoke strongly to me.

This must be a metaphor for something, this process of shaping and illumination, this embellishment of doorways. Who sheds light upon whom? Who jigsaws the raw letters, the original shapes, and who offers the contextualizing shadow, the shifts of light that make meaning legible?

What is this art form called? Ann Zwinger cuts letters and images out of wood and glues them to the various doors at Constant Friendship. She quotes various authors, from Li-Po to St. Bernard, with these shadow letters on doors, painting the text the same color as the background, counting on the natural light to reveal something at the appropriate time—and at other times to obscure. I do the same, I realize. I travel with Ann to her mountain home, her ultimate place of the heart. I take pages of notes, erratic, fragmentary scribblings; a tape recorder captures our conversation; I photograph pieces of the scene. Most of this will never make it into my portrait of Ann for her new statement of conviction and exhortation. I shed light on what I begin to understand, delicately skip what eludes me or what she asks me not to know about her. Ann collects and comments on the details of the world, and I do the same to Ann, performing a secondary natural history.

I travel with Ann to her archival cloister, where she tinkers with the artifacts and manuscripts from a life in the field, cataloging herself. She studies what she used to be, and I observe her as she works. These feel like constant friendships, pairings that are meant to be: the naturalist and nature, the writer and her manuscripts, the scholar and his subject. How like the whimsical and serendipitous interactions of shadow and light, of jigsawed letters and same-colored background, on the doors of a mountain home.

Bibliography of Ann Haymond Zwinger's Work

by Scott Slovic

BOOKS

The Nearsighted Naturalist. Tucson: University of Arizona Press, 1998.

Yosemite: Valley of Thunder. New York: HarperCollins, Tehabi Books, 1998.

Downcanyon: A Naturalist Explores the Colorado River through the Grand Canyon. Tucson: University of Arizona Press, 1995.

With Susan Zwinger. *Women in Wilderness: Writings and Photographs.* New York: Harcourt Brace, Tehabi Books, 1995.

Writing the Western Landscape: Mary Austin and John Muir. Boston: Beacon Press, 1994. Boston: Beacon Press, 1999 (paperback edition).

With Barbara Sparks. *Aspen: Blazon of the West.* Salt Lake City: Peregrine Smith Books, 1991.

Utah II. Portland: Graphic Arts Center Publishing Company, 1990. Portland: Graphic Arts Center Publishing Company, 1999 (paperback edition).

The Mysterious Lands: The Four Deserts of the United States. New York: E. P. Dutton, 1989. New York: E. P. Dutton, 1990 (paperback edition). Tucson:

University of Arizona Press, 1996 (paperback edition).

Colorado II. Portland: Graphic Arts Center Publishing Company, 1987.

John Xántus: The Fort Tejon Letters 1857–1859. Tucson: University of Arizona Press, 1986.

Xántus: The Letters of John Xántus to Spencer Fullerton Baird from San Francisco and Cabo San Lucas, 1859–1861. Baja California Travel Series. Los Angeles: Dawson's Book Shop, 1986.

A Desert Country Near the Sea: The Cape Region of Baja California. New York: Harper and Row, 1983. Tucson: University of Arizona Press, 1987 (paperback edition).

With Edwin Way Teale. *A Conscious Stillness: Two Naturalists on Thoreau's Rivers.* New York: Harper and Row, 1982. Amherst: University of Massachusetts Press, 1984 (paperback edition).

Wind in the Rock: The Canyonlands of Southeastern Utah. New York: Harper and Row, 1978. Tucson: University of Arizona Press, 1986 (paperback edition).

Run, River, Run: A Naturalist's Journey Down One of the Great Rivers of the American West. New York: Harper and Row, 1975. Tucson: University of Arizona Press, 1984 (paperback edition).

With Beatrice E. Willard. *Land Above the Trees: A Guide to American Alpine Tundra.* New York: Harper and Row, 1972. New York: Harper and Row, 1986 (paperback edition). Tucson: University of Arizona Press, 1989 (paperback edition). Boulder, Colo.: Johnson Publishing, 1996 (paperback edition).

Beyond the Aspen Grove. New York: Random House,

1970. New York: Harper and Row, 1981 (paperback edition). Tucson: University of Arizona Press,
1988 (paperback edition).

JOURNAL, MAGAZINE, AND NEWSPAPER PUBLICATIONS

"Human Law/Natural Law: Whose World Is This
Anyway?" *Plateau* 4, no. 1 (Summer 2000): 7–19.

"A Naturalist's Legacy of Caring." *Whole Terrain* 8
(1999/2000): 10–14.

"Island Hopping: Whale's Way." *Islands* 19, no. 1
(February 1999): 130–36.

"The Ghostly Green Light." *Audubon* 101, no. 1
(January/February 1999): 22–27.

"Xántus, John." *American National Biography,* vol. 24
(New York: Oxford University Press, 1999), 97–98.

"Writing the Wild: Landscape in Fiction and Non-
Fiction." Lecture presented April 16, 1998, in the
Wallace Stegner Memorial Lecture Series, then
published. Bozeman: Montana State University,
1999.

"Grand Canyon: Deepening Popularity." *Audubon*
100, no. 6 (November/December 1998): 56–57.

"Who Is Your Favorite Nature Writer?" *Sierra* 83,
no. 5 (June 1998): 92.

"A Journal of the Heart." *Audubon* 99, no. 6
(November/December 1997): 34–35.

"Last Look at the Long River." *Audubon* 99, no. 3
(May/June 1997): 78–86.

"Under the Silver Ceiling." Xerces Society *Wings* 19,
no. 2 (Fall 1996): 14–17.

"It Flows Along Forever." *Orion* 15, no. 3 (Summer
1996): 29–32.

"A Landscape of Memory." *Audubon* 98, no. 3 (May/June 1996): 30–31.

"What Good Is a Desert?" *Audubon* 98, no. 2 (March/April 1996): 40–53, 118–19.

"New Zealand's Kapiti Island Is Strictly for the Birds." *Islands* 16, no. 1 (February 1996): 128–35.

"Is There Anything Down There?" *Orion Society Notebook* 1, no. 1 (Spring/Summer 1995): 8–9.

"Back Home Again." *Nature Conservancy* 45, no. 2 (March/April 1995): 19.

"The Place Where You Live." *Orion* 14, no. 2 (Spring 1995): 25.

"Remembering Indiana." *Audubon* 97, no. 1 (January/February 1995): 105–9.

"A Cave with a View: A Naturalist Robinson Crusoe on the Remote Chilean Island That Set the Stage for Defoe's Novel." *Islands* 13, no. 4 (August 1993): 64–74.

"Of Pebbles and Place." *Audubon* 95, no. 1 (January/February 1993): 92–93.

"What's a Nice Girl Like Me Doing in a Place Like This?" *Western American Literature* 27, no. 2 (Fall 1992): 99–107.

"Writing/Teaching Natural History—A Personal View." *CEA Critic* 54, no. 1 (Fall 1991): 4–11.

"Aspen." *Orion* 10, no. 2 (Spring 1991): 36–41.

"Edward Abbey Eulogy." *Journal of Energy, Natural Resources, and Environmental Law* (January 1990): 26–28.

"Desert Reverie." *Wellesley Alumnae Magazine* 73, no. 2 (Winter 1989): 4–7.

"No Need to Be a Rembrandt." *Reader's Digest* 134, no. 804 (April 1989): 136–38.

"The Best of All Possible Worlds." *Sierra Club Calendar* (1989).

"Writers of the Purple Figwort." *Colorado College Bulletin,* no. 364 (October 1988): 10–11.

"Richard Beidleman." *La Tertulia* 4, no. 2 (Spring 1988): 3.

"First Snowfall." *Colorado College Bulletin,* no. 360 (February 1988): 16–17.

With Julie Jones-Eddy. "In-House Preservation of Early U.S. Government Maps." *Government Publications Review* 15, no. 1 (January/February 1988): 41–47.

"Drawing on Experience." *Orion* 6, no. 1 (Winter 1987): 34–39.

"First Snowfall of Winter." *Springs Magazine* (December 1987): 169–70.

"The Art of Wandering." *Orion* 5, no. 1 (Winter 1986): 4–13.

"A World of Infinite Variety." *Antaeus* 57 (Autumn 1986): 3444.

"A Hungarian in Baja." *Audubon* 87, no. 1 (January 1985): 128–39.

"Becoming Mom to an Infant Word Processor." *Smithsonian* 12, no. 11 (February 1982): 164.

"A'Aly-Waipa." *Audubon* 83, no. 3 (May 1981): 34–42.

". . . A Worthless and Impracticable Region . . ." *Plateau* 52, no. 2 (June 1980): 24–32.

"Browsing: Forty Mountain Acres." Excerpt from *Beyond the Aspen Grove. Chicago Tribune* (October 25, 1979): 4.

"The Flip Side of River Travel." *Adventure Travel* 2, no. 1 (July 1979): 14–21.

"Even the Sky Is Hard." *Audubon* 80, no. 6 (November 1978): 104–18.

"Land of Rock and Wind." *Living Wilderness* 42, no. 142 (July/September 1978): 35–43.

"The Eagle's Fate and Mine Are One." *Audubon* 79, no. 4 (July 1977): 50–88.

"Every Valley Shall Be Exalted and Every Mountain Shall Be Made Low." *Audubon* 78, no. 2 (March 1976): 2–11.

With Dr. Beatrice E. Willard. "The White Mountains." *American West* 9, no. 6 (November 1972): 22–26.

With Dr. Beatrice E. Willard. "Above the Treeline." *Natural History* 81, no. 8 (October 1972): 60–67.

"The Day Before Spring." *Audubon* 74, no. 3 (May 1972): 14–19.

BOOK INTRODUCTIONS

Foreword to *A Journey for All Seasons,* edited by the Nature Conservancy. Rochester, N.Y.: Lyons Press, 2000.

Epilogue to *Traces of Amphibians: A Collection of Classic Natural History,* edited by Gordon Miller. Washington, D.C.: Island Press, 2000.

Foreword to *Into the Field: A Guide to Locally Focused Teaching,* Nature Literacy Series, no. 3. Great Barrington, Mass.: Orion Society, 1999.

Introduction to *Land and Water: The Artists' Point of View,* catalog for the Colorado Springs Fine Arts Center (September 25, 1998 to January 5, 1999). Colorado Springs: Colorado Springs Fine Arts Center, 1998.

Introduction to *A Naturalist Buys an Old Farm,* by Edwin Way Teale. Storrs: University of Connecticut Press, 1998.

Introduction to *The Nearby Faraway,* by David Peterson. Boulder, Colo.: Johnson Books, 1997.

Introduction to *Reading the Forested Landscape,* by
Tom Wessels. Woodstock, Vt.: Countryman Press,
1997.

Introduction to *The Walker's Companion,* by
Elizabeth Ferber and others. New York: Nature
Company/Time-Life Books, 1995.

Introduction to *America,* photographs by Fred
Hirschman. Portland, Oreg.: Graphic Arts Center
Publishing Company, 1994.

Introduction to *The Grand Canyon: Intimate Views,*
by Robert C. Euler and Frank Tikalsky. Tucson:
University of Arizona Press, 1992.

Introduction to *Pueblo, Hardscrabble, Greenhorn,*
by Janet LeCompte. Norman: University of
Oklahoma Press, 1990.

Introduction to *The Sea Around Us,* by Rachel Carson.
New York: Oxford University Press, 1989.

Introduction to *The Local Wilderness: Observing
Neighborhood Nature through an Artist's Eye,* by
Cathy Johnson. New York, N.Y.: Prentice Hall
Press, Phalarope Books, 1987.

Introduction to *The Forgotten Peninsula,* by Joseph
Wood Krutch. Tucson: University of Arizona Press,
1986.

Introduction to *Lightfall and Time,* by Cynthia
Bennet. Flagstaff: Grand Canyon Natural History
Association and Northland Press, 1986.

ANTHOLOGY APPEARANCES

Excerpt from *Downcanyon.* In *Getting Over the Color
Green,* edited by Scott Slovic. Tucson: University
of Arizona Press, 2000.

"From the Lake Rock." In *Progressions: Reading for*

Writers, edited by Betsy Hilbert, 151–55. New York: W. W. Norton, 1998.

"Riversound." In *Writing Down the River,* edited by Kathleen Jo Ryan, 77–81. Flagstaff: Northland Press, 1998.

"Bright Angel Trail: Coda." In *American Nature Writing 1997,* selected by John Murray. San Francisco: Sierra Club, 1997.

"Sidestepping Down Stream." In *Call of the River,* edited by Page Stegner, 69–71. New York: Harcourt Brace, Tehabi Books, 1996.

"Thighbone of a Mouse." In *Testimony: Writers of the West Speak On Behalf of Utah Wilderness*, compiled by Stephen Trimble and Terry Tempest Williams, 32–33. Minneapolis: Milkweed Editions, 1995.

"A Cave with a View: Isla Mas à Tierra, Chile." In *Travelers' Tales: A Woman's World,* edited by Marybeth Bond, 261–65. San Francisco: Travelers' Tales, 1995.

"Back Home Again (Big Darby Creek, Ohio)." In *Heart of the Land: Essays on the Last Great Places,* edited by Joseph Barbata and Lisa Weinerman, 151–60. New York: Pantheon, 1994.

"Space and Place." In *Open Spaces, City Places,* edited by Judy Nolte Temple, 61–69. Tucson: University of Arizona Press, 1994.

"Fort Bottom to Turks Head." In *Being in the World: An Environmental Reader for Writers,* edited by Scott H. Slovic and Terrell F. Dixon, 264–74. New York: Macmillan Publishing Co., 1993.

"Beyond the Aspen Grove." In *The Colorado Book,* edited by Eleanor M. Gehres, Sandra Dallas, Maxine Benton, and Stanley Cuba, 98–100. Golden, Colo.: Fulcrum Publishing, 1993.

"Of Red-Tailed Hawks and Black-Tailed Gnatcatchers." In *Counting Sheep*, edited by Gary Nabhan, 132–54. Tucson: University of Arizona Press, 1993.

"Of White-Winged Doves and Desert Bighorns." In *Celebrating the Land: Women's Nature Writings, 1850–1991*, edited by Carol Knowles, 69–74. Flagstaff: Northland Publishing, 1992.

"Drawing on Experience." In *Finding Home*, edited by Peter Sauer, 239–48. Boston: Beacon Press, 1992.

In *Mother Earth*, edited by Judith Boice, 10, 121. San Francisco: Sierra Club Books, 1992.

"The Mysterious Lands." In *Roger Caras' Treasure of Classic Nature Tales*, edited by Roger Caras, 279–98. New York: Dutton, Truman Talley Books, 1992.

"Waking Up to Eternity." In *The Desert Reader*, edited by Peter Wild, 206–15. Salt Lake City: University of Utah Press, 1991.

"The Streams." In *Late Harvest*, edited by David Pischake, 344–48. New York: Paragon House, 1991.

"A Rinse in the River." In *Sisters of the Earth*, edited by Lorraine Anderson, 47–49. New York: Vintage Books, 1991.

"Gray Rock Canyon at Dawn." In *Things Precious and Wild*, edited by John Terres, 242. Golden, Colo.: Fulcrum Publishing, 1991.

"Of Red-Tailed Hawks and Black-Tailed Gnatcatchers." In *The Norton Book of Nature Writing*, edited by Robert Finch and John Elder, 642–53. New York: W. W. Norton and Company, 1990.

"The Lake Rock." In *Prose and Poetry of the American*

West, edited by James C. Work, 633–42. Lincoln: University of Nebraska Press, 1990.

"A'Aly Waipia." In *Audubon Nature Yearbook,* edited by Les Line, 148–58. Danbury, Conn.: Grolier Books, 1989.

"Greening of Summer." In *Beginnings,* edited by National Wildlife Federation, 36–37. Washington, D.C.: National Wildlife Federation, 1989.

In *Literature and Landscape: Writers of the Southwest,* edited by Cynthia Farah, 100–1, 137. El Paso: Texas Western Press, 1988.

"Becoming Mom to an Infant Word Processor." In *Strategies, A Rhetoric and Reader,* edited by Charlene Tibbetts and A. M. Tibbetts, 335–37. Glenview, Ill.: Scott, Foresman and Company, 1988.

"Cabeza Prieta." In *Words from the Land,* edited by Stephen Trimble, 78–91. Salt Lake City: Peregrine Smith Books, 1988.

"Writers of the Purple Figwort." In *Old Southwest, New Southwest,* edited by Judy Nolte Lensink, 143–54. Tucson: University of Arizona Press, 1987.

"A World of Infinite Variety." In *On Nature,* edited by Daniel Halpern, 33–44. San Francisco: North Point Press, 1987.

"Beyond the Aspen Grove." In *Of Nature and Destiny: An Anthology of American Writers and the American Land,* edited by Robert E. Baron and Elizabeth Junkin, 104–6. Golden, Colo.: Fulcrum, 1986.

"Selecting Descriptive Details." In *Basic Language: Messages and Meanings,* edited by Paulene M. Yates and Edward N. DeLaney, 172. New York: Harper and Row, Publishers, 1983.

SOUND RECORDINGS

Lecture for Peninsula Open Space Trust. Wallace
Stegner Lecture Series, Menlo Park, Calif., May 12,
1999.

Reading from *Downcanyon*. Read by the author on
The Environment Show, hosted by Thomas Lalley.
National Public Radio, April 16, 1996.

Interview and reading from *Downcanyon*. Read by
the author on *Eco-Talk,* hosted by Randy Larsen.
National Public Radio, January 12, 1996.

Interview. *Talk of the Nation: Science Friday,* moderated by Ira Flatow. National Public Radio, May 28,
1993.

The Mysterious Lands. Read by the author. NorthWord
Audio Press, 1993.

Run, River, Run. Read by the author. NorthWord
Audio Press, 1993.

Upcanyon, Downriver: A Naturalist's Journeys. Read by
the author. NorthWord Audio Press, 1993.

"The Wilderness Still Lingers: Passages to Power."
Readings by Western Writers. Tuscon Public
Library and Arizona Humanities Council, 1989.

"Writing Natural History Dialogue #3: Gary Paul
Nabhan and Ann Zwinger," moderated by Edward
Lueders. University of Utah, February 15, 1988.

"Readings," introduced by Lois Shelton. University
of Arizona Poetry Center, November 4, 1987.

"Crowding Around the Waterhole: Environmental
Literature." Readings by Stephen Trimble, Charles
Bowden, Gary Nabhan, and Ann Zwinger. Old
Southwest/New Southwest Conference, Tucson,
November 1985.

"Writers of the Purple Figwort." Speech by author

at Old Southwest/New Southwest Conference, Tucson, November 15, 1985.

"Presidential Address to the Thoreau Society." Thoreau Society Annual Meeting, July 14, 1984.

VIDEO RECORDINGS

Speech and reading. University of Wyoming, Casper, September 14, 1996.

"Visions of Nature: Ann Zwinger." Produced by Letitia Langord in conjunction with Channel Six, Denver, 1994.

INTERVIEWS

Birkhead, Gene. "National Book Award Nominee 'Surprised.'" *Colorado Springs Sun* (April 5, 1993): 11–12.

_____. "Nature Writer Finds True Home in the West." *Colorado Springs Sun* (August 1982).

Borden, Lark. "Head Over Heels in Love with a River." *Colorado Springs Sun* (June 8, 1975): 15–16.

Carlin, Margaret. "Refreshing Descent into the Grand Canyon." *Rocky Mountain News* (November 26, 1995).

Diamonstein, Barbaralee. "Guiding Lights: Women in the Arts." *Ladies Home Journal* 96, no. 5 (May 1979).

DuVal, Linda. "See Level: Meet the Zwingers—And Learn How to See Nature Like You Never Have Before." *Colorado Springs Gazette Telegraph* (August 26, 1999).

_____. "Ann Zwinger: A Woman for All Seasons." *Colorado Springs Gazette Telegraph* (December 18, 1995).

Earle, Jane. "Ecologist-Author Cites Environmental Threat in Colorado." *Denver Post* (June 4, 1970): 23.

Green, Roma. "Successful Artist-Author Finds Forty Is an Adventure." *Colorado Springs Gazette Telegraph* (December 6, 1975): D15.

Harris, Betty. "Violets Were a Favorite Flower of Muncie-Born Colorado Author." *Muncie Evening Press* (May 29, 1970).

Interview. "Catch Colorado." *Vogue* 156, no. 9 (November 15, 1970): 124.

Leuders, Edward. "Field Notes: The Literary Process." *Writing Natural History: Dialogues with Authors*, edited by Edward Leuders. Salt Lake City: University of Utah Press.

Kirchner, Cassie. "An Interview with Ann Zwinger." *Isle* 1, no. 2 (Fall 1993): 123–32.

Millett, Katherine. "Ann Zwinger Outdoors: Quiet Craftsmanship, Creating Space and Suspending Time." *Colorado Springs Sun* (October 22, 1978): 1, 8–10.

Orme, Terry. "Coming Home to the Colorado Plateau." *Salt Lake Tribune* (January 6, 1985).

Porter, William. "River Rapture Writer Celebrates Her Passion for Rushing Water with a Look at the Colorado." *Phoenix Gazette* (October 5, 1995).

Raham, Gary. "Ann Zwinger—A Short Profile." *Guild of Natural Science Illustrators: Colorado Chapter* (January 1985).

Rea, Paul. "An Interview with Ann Zwinger." *Western American Literature* 24, no. 1 (May 1989): 21–36.

Trimble, Stephen. "Ann Zwinger." In *Words from the Land: Encounters with Natural History Writing*, edited by Stephen Trimble, 78–79. Salt Lake City: Peregrine Smith Books, 1988.

BIOGRAPHICAL/CRITICAL STUDIES AND BOOK REVIEWS

Abbey, Edward. "A River for the Living." Review of *Run, River, Run. New York Times Book Review* (October 12, 1975).

Anderson, George. Review of *Wind in the Rock. Evening News* (January 10, 1979).

Armendariz, Sherry. Review of *Downcanyon. Small Press* (February 1996).

Arnold, Stanleigh. "A Naturalist in a Colorado Mountain." Review of *Beyond the Aspen Grove. San Francisco Chronicle* (July 1, 1970).

Atwood, Karen Hoffman. Review of *The Nearsighted Naturalist. Wellesley Alumnae Magazine* 83, no. 4 (Summer 1999).

"Author Shares Refined View of Canyon Sights." *Phoenix Gazette* (October 5, 1995).

"Award Nominee Is Local Author." *Colorado Springs Sun* (March 20, 1973).

Bales, Miriam. "Muncie Author Writes about the Art of Wandering in Nature. Review of *The Nearsighted Naturalist. Muncie Star Press* (April 19, 1999).

_____. "Wild West Brings Out the Best in Hoosier Author in Her Latest . . . Collection of Essays." Review of *The Nearsighted Naturalist. Muncie Star Press* (April 11, 1999).

_____. "Book Is the Next Best Thing to Yosemite Visit." Review of *Yosemite. Muncie Star Press* (August 24, 1997).

_____. "Science in the Hands of a Poet." Review of _Downcanyon. Muncie Star Press_ (November 5, 1995).

_____. "Former Muncie Resident Pens Tribute to High Country Aspen." Review of _Aspen. Muncie Star Press_ (January 19, 1992).

_____. "A Desert View: Naturalist Takes Fond Look at Four Deserts." Review of _The Mysterious Lands. Indianapolis Star_ (October 21, 1990).

_____. "A Lover of the Desert: Muncie-Born Ann Zwinger Writes of Her Excursions in the American Southwest." Review of _The Mysterious Lands. Muncie Star Press_ (April 22, 1990).

_____. "Harsh Beauty and Sharp Contrasts at Baja Tip." Review of _A Desert Country Near the Sea. South Bend Tribune_ (May 27, 1984).

_____. "Thoreau's Rivers Enchanting to Native Hoosiers." Review of _A Conscious Stillness. South Bend Tribune_ (April 29, 1984).

_____. "Muncie Native's Book Recalls _A Desert Country Near the Sea." Muncie Star Press_ (January 29, 1984).

_____. "Ann Zwinger Explores Canyons in Latest Book." Review of _Wind in the Rock. Muncie Star Press_ (January 7, 1979).

_____. "Ann Zwinger's Latest Novel: Journey Down a Great River." Review of _Run, River, Run. Muncie Star Press_ (September 21, 1975).

Beatty, Sarah. "Botanic Gardens Group to See Films." Review of _Beyond the Aspen Grove. Denver Post_ (March 16, 1971).

Barnes, Irston R. "Alpine Flowers in the Summer." Review of _Land Above the Trees. Washington Post_ (March 18, 1973).

Bell, Barbara Currier. Review of *A Desert Country Near the Sea*. *Orion* 3, no. 3 (Summer 1984).

Bigalow, David. "Poetic Adventure in Thoreau Land." Review of *A Conscious Stillness*. *Buffalo News* (September 26, 1982).

Bishop, M. Guy. Review of *John Xántus: The Fort Tejon Letters*. *Californians* (November/December 1987).

Blake, Edgar. Review of *Counting Sheep*. *BioScience* 44, no. 4 (April 1994).

Bonham, Jeanne C. and Roger Bonham. Review of *A Conscious*. *Columbus Sunday Dispatch* (September 5, 1982).

Boxberger, Bob. "Trampled Tundra." *Tacoma News-Tribune* (December 31, 1972).

Brown, Bruce. "The Call of the Wild." Review of *A Desert Country Near the Sea*. *Bookworld* (February 26, 1984).

"Browsing: Forty Mountain Acres." Excerpt from *Beyond the Aspen Grove*. *Chicago Tribune* (October 25, 1979).

Broyles, Bill. Review of *A Desert Country Near the Sea*. *Journal of Arizona History* (Summer 1988).

Bullock, Alice. Review of *Wind in the Rock*. *Los Alamos Monitor* (November 3, 1979).

_____. Review of *Wind in the Rock*. *El Palacio* (Spring 1979).

Burroughs, Mrs. John. Review of *Beyond the Aspen Grove*. *Colorado Gardener* 37, no. 1 (Winter 1971).

Burton, Hal. Review of *Beyond the Aspen Grove*. *Philadelphia Inquirer* (May 31, 1970).

Bush, Monroe. Review of *Land Above the Trees*. *American Forests* (May 1973).

_____. "Hazy, Lazy Days." Review of *Beyond the Aspen Grove*. *American Forests* (July 1970).

Butler, Thomas A. Review of *Land Above the Trees.*
Science Teacher (October 1973).

Cantwell, Robert. "Booktalk: A Rare Mix of Science
and Romance Yields a Classic of Nature Writing."
Review of *Run, River, Run. Sports Illustrated* 44, no.
9 (March 1, 1976).

Carleton, Barbara Oliver. "Ann Haymond Zwinger
'46 and Edmond Way Teale." Review of *A
Conscious Stillness. Wellesley Alumnae Magazine* 67,
no. 3 (Spring 1983).

_____. Review of *Wind in the Rock. Wellesley Alumnae
Magazine* 63, no. 3 (Spring 1979).

Carter, Annetta. Review of *Xántus: The Letters of
John Xántus to Spencer Fullerton Baird from San
Francisco and Cabo San Lucas, 1859–1861.*
Madroño 34, no. 3 (March 1987).

Chandler, Mary Voelz. Review of *The Nearsighted
Naturalist. Boulder Daily Camera* (September 13,
1998).

Chapman, Diane. "Delectable Morsels about Desert
Country." Review of *The Mysterious Lands. Palo
Alto Peninsula Times Tribune* (July 29, 1989).

Clarke, Marion T. "The River Runs On . . . but So
Does the Author." Review of *Run, River, Run.
Baltimore News American* (October 19, 1975).

Cline, Lynn Hunter. "Journal of Downcanyon
Trip Is Consistently Magnificent." Review of
Downcanyon. New Mexican (October 22, 1995).

Cohen, Michael P. Review of *Wind in the Rock.
Western American Literature* 14, no. 3 (Fall 1979).

Commire, Anne. "Zwinger, Ann 1925." *Something
about the Author: Facts and Pictures about Authors
and Illustrators of Books for Young People.* Vol. 46,

edited by Anne Commire. Detroit: Gale Research, 1987.

Cross, Bill. Review of *Downcanyon*. *Paddler* (August 1996).

Davisson, Peter. "The Journals and Journeys of Henry David Thoreau." Review of *A Conscious Stillness*. *Washington Post Book World* (November 7, 1982).

Delaney-Lehman, Maureen. Review of *The Nearsighted Naturalist*. *Library Journal* 123, no. 18 (November 1, 1998).

_____. "Writings and Writers on the Aesthetics of Nature." *Wilson Library Bulletin* 69 (April 1995).

Diehl, Digby. "Big Gift Books of the Season Offer Armchair Holidays." Review of *A Desert Country Near the Sea*. *Los Angeles Herald Examiner* (December 14, 1983).

Dieter, William. Review of *The Mysterious Lands*. *Smithsonian* 20, no. 12 (March 1990).

DuCruc, Jean Pierre. Review of *Land Above the Trees*. *Le Naturaliste Canadien* 100 (1973).

Dunning, John B. Review of *Downcanyon*. *North American Bird Banders* 21, no. 3 (February 1997).

DuVal, Linda. "An Eye for Nature's Intricate Detail." Review of *The Nearsighted Naturalist*. *Colorado Springs Gazette Telegraph* (October 11, 1998).

_____. "Zwinger's 'River' Now in Paperback." Review of *Run, River, Run*. *Colorado Springs Gazette Telegraph* (December 1, 1984).

_____. "Binding Nature: Naturalist Ann Zwinger Blends Pictures, Words." Review of *A Conscious Stillness*. *Colorado Springs Gazette Telegraph* (October 9, 1982).

Eastburn, Kathryn. "Going Natural." Review of *The*

Nearsighted Naturalist. Colorado Springs Independent (September 30, 1998–October 6, 1998).

"Ecologist-Author to 'Focus on *Land Above the Trees'* in Alpine Tundra Talk Oct. 4." *Denver Post* (September 27, 1973).

English, T. J. Review of *Downcanyon: A Naturalist Explores the Colorado River Through the Grand Canyon. Audubon* 98, no. 1 (January/February 1996).

Farley, Cory. Review of *The Mysterious Lands. Reno Gazette Journal* (October 2, 1989).

Fetler, John. "Current Books." Review of *Run, River, Run. Colorado Springs Gazette Telegraph* (June 22, 1975).

_____. "Current Books." Review of *Land Above the Trees. Colorado Springs Gazette Telegraph* (November 12, 1972).

_____. "Current Books." Review of *Beyond the Aspen Grove. Colorado Springs Gazette Telegraph* (May 24, 1970).

Fine, Cathy. "'Downcanyon' Takes Reader on Journey of Colorado River." *Herald Valley (Ariz.) Window* (March 23–24, 1996).

Flower, Dean. "Nature Does Not Exist for Us." *Review of The Nearsighted Naturalist. Hudson Review* 52, no. 2 (Summer 1999).

Fontana, B. L. Review of *John Xántus: The Fort Tejon Letters. Books of the Southwest* 335 (October 1986).

_____. Review of *Run, River, Run. Books of the Southwest* 317 (April 1985).

_____. Review of *A Desert Country Near the Sea. SMRC Newsletter* 18, no. 59 (September 1984).

Fosberg, F. R. Review of *Land Above the Trees*. *Biological Conservation* 5, no. 4 (October 1973).

Fowler, Carol. Review of *Wind in the Rock*. *Contra Costa* (April 1, 1970).

Freshwater, Philip C. "A Private World." Review of *Land Above the Trees*. *Sacramento Bee* (June 14, 1970).

Gabrielson, Ira N. Review of *Land Above the Trees*. *Living Wilderness* 37, no. 122 (Summer 1973).

"Gallery A and Taos Bookshop to Host Reception for Zwinger Show." Review of *Beyond the Aspen Grove*. *Taos News* (July 9, 1970).

Garrelick, Renee. "Bewitched by the Assabet." Review of *A Conscious Stillness*. *Concord Journal* (July 22, 1982).

Garstka, Katharine Galloway. Review of *The Mysterious Lands*. *Library Journal* 114, no. 6 (April 1, 1989).

_____. Review of *A Desert Country Near the Sea*. *Library Journal* 108, no. 15 (September 1, 1983).

Gerhardt, Gary. "A Naturalist's Look at Constant Friendship in the Rampart Range." Review of *Beyond the Aspen Grove*. *Long Beach Press Telegram* (July 16, 1970).

Goodrich, Chris. Review of *Downcanyon*. *Los Angeles Times Book Review* (September 10, 1995).

Gordon, Alexander. Review of *Land Above the Trees* and *Beyond the Aspen Grove*. *Western American Literature* 7 (1972).

Gordon, Joe. "A Naturalist's Enterprise: Some Thoughts on Ann Zwinger's *Downcanyon*." *La Tertulia* (Colorado College) 12, no. 2 (Spring 1996).

Gorra, Michael. Review of *Downcanyon*. *New York Times Book Review* (December 3, 1995).

Hall, Elizabeth. Review of *Land Above the Trees*. *Library Journal* 98, no. 3 (January 15, 1973).

Hall, George A. Review of *John Xántus: The Fort Tejon Letters*. *Wilson Bulletin* (1987).

Hancock, Judith. "A Pair of Guides to Lesser-Known Wonders of Nature." *Maine Sunday Telegraph* (November 23, 1986).

Hanson, Roseann. Review of *Downcanyon*. *Desert Skies* (Winter 1995).

"Hardcovers in Brief." *Washington Post Book World* (July 23, 1989).

Harding, Walter. Review of *A Conscious Stillness*. *Orion Nature Quarterly* 1, no. 3 (Autumn 1982).

Harris, Karen. Review of audiotape of *Upcanyon, Downriver*. *Booklist* 89, no. 2 (September 15, 1992).

Hart Jr., C. W. Review of *Wind in the Rock*. *Smithsonian* 9, no. 11 (February 1979).

Harvey, Miles. Review of *Downcanyon*. *Outside* 21, no. 1 (January 1996).

Havlick, R. J. "American Nature Writers." *Choice* 34, no. 8 (April 1997).

Hay, John. "The Wilderness: Setting Its Own Terms for the Human Body and Spirit." Includes review of *Run, River, Run*. *Harvard Magazine* (September 1975).

Hayes, E. Nelson. "Late Spring-Summer Titles." Review of *A Conscious Stillness*. *Bookcast* (June 28, 1982–July 5, 1982).

Hedgpeth, Joel W. Review of *John Xántus: The Fort Tejon Letters*. *Quarterly Review of Biology* (June 1987).

_____. Review of *A Desert Country Near the Sea. Oceans* 17, no. 60 (July 1984).

Herbert, Gary N. Review of *Beyond the Aspen Grove. American West* 7, no. 5 (September 1970).

Herd, Shirley. "Awesome Beauty of the Baja California Desert." Review of *A Desert Country Near the Sea. San Diego Union* (January 22, 1984).

Hewes, Jeremy Joan. Review of *Run, River, Run. Western Letter* (June 1975).

Hickey, Pat. Review of *A Conscious Stillness. New Age* (November 1982).

Hinton, Harwood P. Review of *Xántus: The Letters of John Xántus to Spencer Fullerton Baird from San Francisco and Cabo San Lucas, 1859–1861. Southern California Quarterly* 70 (Fall 1988).

Hollenbeck, Ralph. Review of *A Conscious Stillness. Living Today* (September 26, 1982).

Holmgren, Noel H. Review of *Wind in the Rock. Garden Magazine* (Journal of the New York Botanic Gardens) (March/April 1979).

Horton, Charles. "Two Naturalists on Thoreau's Rivers." Review of *A Conscious Stillness. Chapel Hill Newspaper* (July 25, 1982).

Houston, C. Stuart. Review of *John Xántus: The Fort Tejon Letters. North American Bird Banders* 1, no. 12 (April/June 1987).

Howard, Enid C. Review of *Run, River, Run. Wilderness Camping* (December 1975).

Howard, Jennifer. "Paperbacks." *Washington Post Book World* (April 25, 1999).

Hughes, Jeremy Jones. Review of *Run, River, Run. Western Letters* (June 1975).

Huntington, Lee Pennock. Review of *A Conscious Stillness. Country Journal* (July 1982).

Hupp, Jim. Review of *Beyond the Aspen Grove. Berkeley Freedom News* (November 1970).

Husband, Susan. "Pressed Pages: Announcing a Good Read for Desert Aficionados." *Plant Press* 14, no. 1 (Spring 1990).

Huser, Verne. Review of *Downcanyon. Western American Literature* 31, no. 1 (May 1996).

Hutchison, W. H. Review of *Wind in the Rock. San Francisco Chronicle* (May 22, 1979).

"Indiana Authors Honored." *Bloomington Herald-Telegraph* (April 19, 1971).

Isaacson, Richard T. Review of *A Desert Country Near the Sea. Garden Center Bulletin* (July 1984).

Ives, J. D. "Deep in the Tundra." Review of *Land Above the Trees. Arctic and Alpine Research* 5, no. 2 (Spring 1973).

Jacobson, Ethel. "Nature's Shining Moments." Review of *A Conscious Stillness. St. Louis Post Dispatch* (September 26, 1982).

James, Peggy. "Ecological Book Opens Vistas for Authoress." *Colorado Springs Gazette Telegraph* (June 7, 1970).

Jarvis, P. J. Review of *Land Above the Trees. Ecological Abstracts* 9 (1990).

Jenkins, Dale W. Review of *Land Above the Trees. Smithsonian* 3, no. 11 (February 1973).

Jennings, John. "A Grand Read." Review of *Downcanyon. Tucson Citizen* (September 22, 1995).

Johnson, Thurman E. "Readers' Realm: Cherished Gift Found in Books." Review of *Wind in the Rock. Fort Wayne News-Sentinel* (December 2, 1978).

Jones, Julia. "Five Make Canyon Life's Work Grand Revelations." Review of *Wind in the Rock. Arizona*

Republic/Phoenix Gazette, southeast edition (April 6, 1989).

Jones, Vard. "Five Canyons Play Role in Naturalist's Study." Review of *Wind in the Rock. Salt Lake City Tribune* (February 11, 1979).

"Just Browsing." Excerpts from *Beyond the Aspen Grove. Chicago Tribune* (October 25, 1970).

Keister, Don A. Review of *A Conscious Stillness. Cleveland Plain Dealer* (November 21, 1982).

Keppler, Joseph. "Audiobooks." *Booklist* 90, no. 10 (January 15, 1994).

Kleiner, Dick. "Autumn Brings Desert to Life." Review of *The Mysterious Lands. Palm Springs Desert Sun* (September 9, 1989).

Klimley, Susan. Review of *A Conscious Stillness. Library Journal* 107 (August 1982).

Knoblauch, Eugene R. "On the Tundra." Review of *Land Above the Trees. Wilmington News* (January 10, 1993).

Korach, Karen A. *Third International Exhibition of Botanical Art and Illustration Catalogue.* Pittsburg: Hunt Institute for Botanical Documentation, Carnegie-Mellon University, 1972.

Krentz, Doug. "Writing, Rafting on the Colorado." *Arizona Daily Star* (September 26, 1995).

Ladner, Mildred. "World of Books: Books on West Give Feeling of Travel." Review of *Wind in the Rock. Tulsa World* (November 12, 1978).

Laird, David. "Southwest's Best Books of '95." Review of *Downcanyon. Arizionia Daily Star* (December 17, 1995).

_____. Review of *Downcanyon. Books of the Southwest* 39, no. 11 (November 1995).

_____. Review of *The Mysterious Lands. Books of the Southwest* 372 (November 1989).

Langford, Dale. "Greenery Books Make a Great Gardener's Gift." *Rocky Mountain News* (December 21, 1991).

Latimer, Ruth. "In All Seasons." Review of *Beyond the Aspen Grove. Cincinnati Enquirer* (July 23, 1970).

LeGuin, Ursula. "Some See Nature, Some Feel It." Review of *Writing the Western Landscape. Oregonian* (October 28, 1994).

Lehman, Tony. Review of *Xántus: The Letters of John Xántus to Spencer Fullerton Baird from San Francisco and Cabo San Lucas, 1859–1861. Branding Iron* (Los Angeles Corral) 172 (Summer 1988).

Lilliard, Richard G. "Exploring the Nature of the Baja Cape." Review of *A Desert Country Near the Sea. Los Angeles Times Book Review* (December 13, 1983).

Long, Carol S. Review of *A Desert Country Near the Sea. Western Literature Association* 19, no. 4 (Fall 1988).

Long, John. "A Naturalist Point of View." Review of *A Conscious Stillness. Providence Sunday Journal* (January 16, 1983).

Lucia, Elklis. "Western Americana: Cowboys As Homosexuals?" Review of *Wind in the Rock. Oregonian* (March 25, 1979).

Lueloff, Jorie. "Canoeing, Climbing, Conquering." Review of *Run, River, Run. Chicago Tribune* (July 13, 1975).

Lyon, Thomas J. "Sketches, Photos, and Sermons." Review of *The Mysterious Lands. Sierra* 73, no. 3 (1990).

Martin, J. C. "Southwestern Books to Savor." Review

of *The Mysterious Lands. Arizona Daily Star* (December 17, 1989).

Martinez, Fabio A. Review of *Xántus: The Letters of John Xántus to Spencer Fullerton Baird from San Francisco and Cabo San Lucas, 1859–1861. Journal of San Diego History* 34 (Summer 1988).

Matthews, Steve. Review of *Plants in Danger. School Library Journal* 26, no. 6 (February 1980).

McAdow, Ron. "The Naturalists' River." Review of *A Conscious Stillness. Sanctuary* (Journal of the Massachusetts Audubon Society) (September/ October 1993).

McFadden, Ruth Mauzy. Review of *Land Above the Trees. Muncie Evening Press* (April 24, 1973).

McLure, John W. Review of *Downcanyon. Science Activities* (Summer 1996).

McNulty, Deirdre. Illustrations for "How and Where to Ride Our Rivers." *National Parks* (March/April 1985).

Meixsell, Anne Bruch. Review of *The Mysterious Lands. Wellesley Alumnae Magazine* 74, no. 2 (Winter 1990).

Metheny, Dorothy. Review of *Run, River, Run. Bulletin of the American Rock Garden Society* 33, no. 4 (Fall 1975).

Metzger, Linda. "Zwinger, Ann 1925." *Contemporary Authors.* New Revision Series, vol. 13, edited by Linda Metzger. Detroit: Gale Research, 1984.

Mighetto, Lisa. Review of *John Xántus: The Fort Tejon Letters. Western Historical Quarterly* 18, no. 2 (April 1987) 223.

Miguy, Bishop. Review of *John Xántus: The Fort Tejon Letters. Californians* (November/December 1987).

Millett, Katherine. *"Wind in the Rock . . .* A Canyonland Reverie." *Colorado Springs Sun* (October 22, 1978).

Milne, Lorus J. Review of *A Desert Country Near the Sea. Explorers Journal* 63, no. 2 (November 25, 1983).

Moeckel, Nancy. Review of *Downcanyon. Library Journal* 120, no. 13 (August 1995).

Muir, Myra. "Award Winners Focus on Environment." Review of *Downcanyon. Oregonian* (November 19, 1995).

Muncie, John. "Enamored of Itsy Bitsy Spiderlings." Review of *Downcanyon. Los Angeles Times* (September 24, 1995).

Murray, John. Review of *Downcanyon. Bloomsbury Review* (September/October 1995).

Nabhan, Gary. "Narrative of a Naturalist." *Bloomsbury Review* (October 1984).

_____. Review of *Run, River, Run. American West* 13, no. 6 (November/December 1976).

_____. Review of *Wind in the Rock. American West* 16, no. 4 (July/August 1979).

Neal, Arminta. Review of *Run, River, Run. Washington D.C. Museum News* (November/December 1976).

Needham, George. Review of *Downcanyon. Booklist* 92, no. 6 (November 15, 1995).

Norton, Alice. Review of *Beyond the Aspen Grove. Wellesley Alumnae Magazine* 57, no. 1 (Autumn 1972).

Noyes, Judith. Review of *Beyond the Aspen Grove. Chinook News* (Summer 1970).

Nygaard, Anita. Review of *Beyond the Aspen Grove. Library Journal* 95, no. 13 (July 1, 1970).

Olson, Mary Ruth. "Thoreau Revisited." Review of *A*

Conscious Stillness. McAllen *(Tex.) Monitor* (February 6, 1983).

Pivoda, Shiloh Richter. Review of *The Nearsighted Naturalist*. *Books of the Southwest* 42.4, no. 468 (Fall 1998).

Pober, Stacy. Review of audiotape of *The Mysterious Lands*. *Library Journal* 119, no. 2 (February 1, 1994).

Porter, Charlotte M. Review of *John Xántus: The Fort Tejon Letters*. *Isis* 77, no. 289 (December 1986).

Porter, Joseph C. Review of *John Xántus: The Fort Tejon Letters*. *New Mexico Historical Review* (July 1988).

Porter, William. "River Rapture Writer Celebrates Her Passion for Rushing Water with a Look at the Colorado." Review of *Downcanyon*. *Phoenix Gazette* (October 5, 1995).

Powell, Lawrence Clark. Review of *A Desert Country Near the Sea*. *Books of the Southwest* 304 (March 1984).

Pride, George H. Review of *Land Above the Trees*. *Arnoldia* 34, no. 6 (November/December 1974).

Prouty, Dick. "Like High Country? 'Land Above' a Must." Review of *Land Above the Trees*. *Denver Post* (December 31, 1972).

Pyle, Robert Michael. "Wit, Whimsy, and Wonder." Review of *The Nearsighted Naturalist*. *Oregonian* (October 12, 1988).

_____. Review of *Land Above the Trees*. *American West* 10, no. 4 (July 1973).

Ravitz, Abe C. Review of *Run, River, Run*. *Cleveland Plain Dealer* (June 22, 1975).

Rawls, James J. Review of *John Xántus: The Fort Tejon Letters*. *Pacific Historical Review* 57, no. 1 (February 1988).

Reichholf, Joseph H. Review of *A Desert Country Near the Sea. Studies on Neotropical Fauna and Environment* (Netherlands) 21, no. 4 (1986).

Review of *Writing the Western Landscape. Washington Post Book World* (April 25, 1999).

Review of *The Nearsighted Naturalist. Weekly Alibi* (November 17, 1998).

Review of *The Nearsighted Naturalist. Denver Post* (November 1, 1998).

Review of *The Nearsighted Naturalist. Audubon* 100, no. 5 (September/October 1998).

Review of *The Nearsighted Naturalist. Rocky Mountain News* (September 13, 1998).

Review of *The Nearsighted Naturalist. Publishers Weekly* 245, no. 30 (July 27, 1998).

Review of *The Nearsighted Naturalist. Kirkus Reviews* (July 1, 1998).

Review of *Downcanyon. Book Talk* (New Mexico Book League) 25, no. 3 (June 1996).

Review of *Downcanyon. New York Times Book Review* (December 3, 1995).

Review of *Downcanyon. Colorado Springs Independent* (December, 1995).

Review of *Downcanyon. Arizona Adventure* (October 19, 1995).

Review of *Downcanyon. Los Angeles Times* (September 10, 1995).

Review of *Downcanyon. International Rivers Network* (August/September 1995).

Review of *Downcanyon. Kirkus Reviews* (August 15, 1995).

Review of *Downcanyon. Publishers Weekly* 242, no. 33 (August14, 1995).

Review of *Writing the Western Landscape. Oregonian* (October 23, 1994).

Review of *Writing the Western Landscape. Library Journal* 119, no. 16 (October 1, 1994).

Review of *Writing the Western Landscape. Publishers Weekly* 241, no. 29 (July 18, 1994).

Review of *Land Above the Trees. Library Journal* 117, no. 15 (September 15, 1992).

Review of audiotape of *Upcanyon, Downriver. Publishers Weekly* 239, no. 30 (July 6, 1992).

Review of *The Mysterious Lands. Talking Book Topics* (November/December 1990).

Review of *Run, River, Run. Natural History Book Services* (Autumn 1990).

Review of *Land Above the Trees. Phytologia* 68, no. 3 (March 1990).

Review of *The Mysterious Lands. SMRC Newsletter* 24, no. 82 (March 1990).

Review of *The Mysterious Lands. Smithsonian* 20, no. 12 (March 1990).

Review of *Land Above the Trees. Small Press Book Review* (January/February 1990).

Review of *Land Above the Trees. Wildlife Book Review* (December 1989).

Review of *Land Above the Trees. Sierra* 74, no. 6 (November/December 1989).

Review of *Land Above the Trees. Phytologia* 67, no. 11 (November 1989).

Review of *Land Above the Trees. Reference and Research Book News* (October 1989).

Review of *The Mysterious Lands. Kirkus Reviews* (March 1, 1989).

Review of *The Mysterious Lands. Publishers Weekly* 236, no. 6 (February 10, 1989).

Review of *A Desert Country Near the Sea. Literate Traveler* (July 1988).

Review of *A Desert Country Near the Sea. Arizona Daily Star* (April 10, 1988).

Review of *A Desert Country Near the Sea. Latin America in Books* (July 1987).

Review of *Land Above the Trees. National Wetlands Newsletter* (May/June 1987).

Review of *Run, River, Run. Sunset Magazine* 178, no. 3 (March 1987).

Review of *A Conscious Stillness. Phytologia* 61, no. 5 (December 1986).

Review of *Run, River, Run. High Country News* 18, no. 21 (November 10, 1986).

Review of *John Xántus: The Fort Tejon Letters. SMRC Newsletter* 20, no. 68 (November 1986).

Review of *John Xántus: The Fort Tejon Letters. Pacific Historian* (Fall 1986).

Review of *John Xántus: The Fort Tejon Letters. Bloomsbury Review* (July/August 1986).

Review of *Run, River, Run. Arizona Daily Star* (September 22, 1985).

Review of *Run, River, Run. Washington Post Book World* (March 3, 1985).

Review of *Run, River, Run. New York Times Book Review* (December 23, 1984).

Review of *A Desert Country Near the Sea. Garden Center Bulletin* (July 1984).

Review of *A Desert Country Near the Sea. Journal of the San Diego Historical Society* (Summer 1984).

Review of *A Desert Country Near the Sea. Costa Mesa (Calif.) Waterfront* (April 1984).

Review of *A Desert Country Near the Sea. Books of the Southwest* 304 (March 1984).

Review of *A Desert Country Near the Sea. Choice* 21, no. 7 (March 1984).

Review of *A Desert Country Near the Sea. Latin America in Books* (January 1984).

Review of *A Desert Country Near the Sea. Detroit Free Press* (December 4, 1983).

Review of *A Desert Country Near the Sea. Publishers Weekly* 230, no. 41 (October 14, 1983).

Review of *A Desert Country Near the Sea. Library Journal* 108, no. 15 (September 1, 1983).

Review of *A Conscious Stillness. Booklist* (August 1982).

Review of *A Conscious Stillness. Publishers Weekly* 221, no. 25 (June 18, 1982).

Review of *Wind in the Rock. Orion Nature Books* 2, no. 1 (January 1980).

Review of *Wind in the Rock. Arizona Daily Star* (December 23, 1979).

Review of *Wind in the Rock. Oregonian* (March 25, 1979).

Review of *Wind in the Rock. Progressive* 43 (March 1979).

Review of *Wind in the Rock. Horn Book Magazine* 55 (February 1979).

Review of *Wind in the Rock. Trenton Times* (December 5, 1978).

Review of *Wind in the Rock. Fort Wayne News-Sentinel* (December 2, 1978).

Review of *Wind in the Rock. Albemarle (N.C.) Stanley News and Press* (November 24, 1978).

Review of *Wind in the Rock. Tulsa World* (November 12, 1978).

Review of *Wind in the Rock. Book Talk* (New Mexico League) 7, no. 5 (November 1978).

Review of *Beyond the Aspen Grove. Colorado Springs Sun* (October 22, 1978).

Review of *Wind in the Rock. Library Journal* 103, no. 17 (October 1, 1978).

Review of *Wind in the Rock. Publishers Weekly* 214, no. 8 (August 21, 1978).

Review of *Wind in the Rock. Science News* 115 (1978).

Review of *Run, River, Run. Washington D.C. Museum News* (November/December 1976).

Review of *Run, River, Run. Baltimore News American* (October 19, 1975).

Review of *Run, River, Run. Chicago Booklist* (September 1, 1975).

Review of *Run, River, Run. Booklist: Books for Young Adults* 71, no. 1 (September 1, 1975).

Review of *Run, River, Run. Hartford Courant* (August 31, 1975).

Review of *Run, River, Run. Pacific Sun Literary Quarterly* (August 21, 1975).

Review of *Run, River, Run. Erie (Pa.) Times* (August 11, 1975).

Review of *Run, River, Run. Booklist* 71, no. 1 (September 1, 1975).

Review of *Run, River, Run. Fort Worth Morning Star-Telegraph* (July 20, 1975).

Review of *Run, River, Run. Cleveland Plain Dealer* (June 22, 1975).

Review of *Run, River, Run. Colorado Springs Sun* (June 8, 1975).

Review of *Run, River, Run. Western Letter* (June 1975).

Review of *Run, River, Run. Library Journal* 100, no. 10 (May 15, 1975).

Review of *Run, River, Run. Publishers Weekly* 222, no. 33 (April 14, 1975).

Review of *Run, River, Run. Denver Post* (April 4, 1975).

Review of *Run, River, Run. Kirkus Reviews* (April 1, 1975).

Review of *Land Above the Trees. Indiana Alumni Magazine* 37, no. 5 (January/February 1975).

Review of *Land Above the Trees. Backpacker Book List* (Spring 1974).

Review of *Land Above the Trees. Book Review Digest* (October 7, 1973).

Review of *Land Above the Trees. Denver Post* (October 7, 1973).

Review of *Land Above the Trees. Science Teacher* (October 1973).

Review of *Land Above the Trees. Bulletin of the American Rock Garden Society* (July 1973).

Review of *Land Above the Trees. American Artist* (June 1973).

Review of *Land Above the Trees. Palo Alto Times* (May 12, 1973).

Review of *Land Above the Trees. Redwood City* (May 12, 1973).

Review of *Land Above the Trees. Choice* 10, no. 3 (May 1973).

Review of *Land Above the Trees. Washington Post* (March 18, 1973).

Review of *Land Above the Trees. Santa Monica Outlook* (February 3, 1973).

Review of *Land Above the Trees. Long Beach Independent* (January 31, 1973).

Review of *Land Above the Trees. Library Journal* 98, no. 1 (January 15, 1973).

Review of *Land Above the Trees. Denver Post* (December 31, 1972).

Review of *Land Above the Trees. Louisville Courier-Journal* (December 10, 1972).

Review of *Land Above the Trees. Colorado Springs Sun* (December 3, 1972).

Review of *Land Above the Trees. Colorado Springs Gazette Telegraph* (November 12, 1972).

Review of *Land Above the Trees. Publishers Weekly* 219, no. 35 (September 18, 1972).

Review of *Beyond the Aspen Grove. Colorado Springs Sun* (September 22, 1971).

Review of *Beyond the Aspen Grove. Choice* 7, no. 7 (September 1970).

Review of *Beyond the Aspen Grove. San Francisco Chronicle* (July 1, 1970).

Review of *Beyond the Aspen Grove. Long Beach Independent* (June 16, 1970).

Review of *Beyond the Aspen Grove. Long Beach Press Telegraph* (June 16, 1970).

Review of *Beyond the Aspen Grove. Sacramento Bee* (June 14, 1970).

Review of *Beyond the Aspen Grove. Northeast Mall* (June 10, 1970).

Review of *Beyond the Aspen Grove. Denver Post* (June 4, 1970).

Review of *Beyond the Aspen Grove. Philadelphia Inquirer* (May 31, 1970).

Review of *Beyond the Aspen Grove. Publishers Weekly* 197, no. 13 (March 31, 1970).

Review of *Beyond the Aspen Grove. Publishers Weekly* 197, no. 10 (March 9, 1970).

Richmond, Dick. Review of audiotape of *The*

Mysterious Lands. St. Louis Post-Dispatch (February 24, 1994).

Rifkin, Ira. "A Loving Look at Beautiful Baja." Review of *A Desert Country Near the Sea. Los Angeles Daily News* (November 27, 1983).

Ronald, Ann. "Kingdom, Phylum, Class, Order: Twentieth-Century American Nature Writer." Includes review of *The Mysterious Lands. Western American Literature* 33, no. 4 (Winter 1999).

_____. "Raising the Bar." Review of *The Nearsighted Naturalist. Western American Literature* 34, no. 1 (Spring 1999).

Rosen, Susan. "American Alps Pictured, Described in New Book." Review of *Land Above the Trees. Taos News* (December 13, 1972).

Rubin, Merle. "Meticulous, Lyrical Look at Nature in Baja." Review of *A Desert Country Near the Sea. Christian Science Monitor* (February 3, 1984).

Rudolph, Emanuel D. "Naturally Good Writers Wild about the Land." *Columbus Dispatch* (May 8, 1988).

Ruppe, John. "Tracing a Great River's Wild Course." Review of *Run, River, Run. Christian Science Monitor* (July 2, 1975).

Sanford, Susan. "A Song for the Other California: Ann Zwinger's *A Desert Country Near the Sea* Brings the Remote Cape Region of Baja California into Reach." *Pacific Discovery* 37, no. 4 (October/December 1984).

Sankey, John. Review of *A Desert Country Near the Sea. Journal of Arid Environments* (England) (October 1987).

Sarton, May. "Did You Know Bees Like Blue? *Beyond*

the Aspen Grove." *New York Times Book Review*
(July 12, 1970).

Schmidt, Rudolf. Review of *A Desert Country Near the
Sea. Taxon* 42 (August 1993).

Scratch, Walter. Review of *Land Above the Trees. Santa
Monica Outlook* (February 3, 1973).

Shaw, Mildred Hart. Review of *Wind in the Rock.
Grand Junction Sentinel* (November 19, 1978).

Shaw, Phyllis. Review of *Beyond the Aspen Grove.
Sanford Tribune* (August 13, 1970).

Shotwell, Robert. "Book Notes: Tales of Escape from
City Life." Review of *Wind in the Rock. Arizona
Republic* (October 29, 1978).

"Six Recent Books on the 'Spiritual Heart of the
West.'" Review of *Run, River, Run. Sunset* 178
(March 1987).

Sledge, Broox. Review of *A Desert Country Near the
Sea. Deer Creek (Miss.) Pilot* (October 20, 1983).

Slovic, Scott. "Giving Expression to Nature: Voices of
Environmental Literature." *Environment* 41, no. 2
(March 1999).

Smith, Karen Sue. "Books: Critics' Choices for
Christmas." Review of *The Mysterious Lands.
Commonweal* 116, no. 21 (December 1, 1989).

Smith, Robert E. Review of *Land Above the Trees.
Journal of the West* 13 (January 1974).

Smyth, Ed. "A Thorny and Arid Experience." Review
of *A Desert Country Near the Sea. San Francisco
Chronicle* (April 15, 1984).

Sokoll, Judy. Review of *Women in Wilderness. School
Library Journal* 41, no. 12 (December, 1995).

Sorgenfrei, Robert. Review of *The Mysterious Lands.
Books of the Southwest* 372 (November 1989).

"Special Programs Lined Up for Nature Center's

Twenty-fifth Year: Storyteller, Nature Author Featured." *Cincinnati Post* (March 26, 1991).

"Springs Author Wins Book Award." *Rocky Mountain News* (September 12, 1995).

Stanley, Daray. "Going with the Flow." Review of *Run, River, Run. Pacific Sun Literary Quarterly* (August 21, 1975).

Stuttaford, Genevieve. Review of *The Mysterious Lands. Publishers Weekly* 235, no. 6 (Februrary 10, 1989).

_____. Review of *A Desert Country Near the Sea. Publishers Weekly* 224, no. 38 (October 14, 1983).

Sunder, John E. Review of *John Xántus: The Fort Tejon Letters. Journal of San Diego History* 33 (Winter 1978).

Tallmadge, John. Review of *Writing the Western Landscape: Mary Austin and John Muir. Orion* 14, no. 1 (Winter 1995).

Thompson, Gerald. Review of *John Xántus: The Fort Tejon Letters. Southern California Quarterly* 69 (Spring 1987).

Tomeo, Richard W. "Green River Rhapsody." Review of *Run, River, Run. Hartford Courant* (August 31, 1975).

Tweit, Susan J. "Naturalist Ambles Far from Home." Review of *The Nearsighted Naturalist. Albuquerque Journal* (February 21, 1999).

"Two Talents, One Woman in Taos." *New Mexican* (December 3, 1972).

"University of Arizona Press Reprints Naturalist Zwinger's Book." Review of *Wind in the Rock. Lo Que Pasa* (August 15, 1986).

VanderMeulen, Joe. Review of *The Nearsighted Naturalist. Forword* 1, no. 4 (September 1998).

Vington, L. Review of *Run, River, Run. Fort Worth Morning Star-Telegraph* (July 20, 1975).

Walden, Monica L. Review of *Run, River, Run. Library Journal* 100, no. 10 (May 15, 1975).

Wanner, Irene. Review of *Downcanyon. Seattle Times* (December 24, 1995).

Weinstein, Frances. Review of audiotape of *Upcanyon, Downriver. Library Journal* 117, no. 17 (October 15, 1992).

Wellejus, Ed. "Travel Books." Review of *Run, River, Run. Erie (Pa.) Times* (August 11, 1975).

White, Fred D. "Nature: The Intimate, Outside of Culture." Review of *Run, River, Run. Minneapolis Tribune* (October 5, 1975).

"Why We Need Hard Times." Excerpt from *The Mysterious Lands. New York Times Book Review* (November 18, 1990).

Wild, Peter. "Ann Zwinger." *American Nature Writers*, edited by John Elder. New York: Charles Scribner's Sons, 1996.

_____. *Ann Zwinger.* Western Writers Series, no. 111. Boise, Idaho: Boise State University, 1993.

_____. "A Colorado River Bookshelf." *High Country News* 18, no. 21 (November 10, 1986).

_____. Review of *John Xántus: The Fort Tejon Letters. Arizona and the West* (Autumn 1986).

_____. "The Seeing 'I.' Recent Nature Writing in the West." *Bloomsbury Review* (July/August 1986).

_____. "Wandering the Other California." Review of *A Desert Country Near the Sea. Sierra* 69, no. 90 (March/April 1984).

Williams, Paul. "When Writers Read." Review of *A Conscious Stillness. Christian Science Monitor* (August 8, 1983).

Willis, Truman. Review of *Wind in the Rock*. *Wichita Falls Times* (January 7, 1979).

Wingfield, Andrew. Review of *Writing the Western Landscape*. *Amicus Journal* 21, no. 4 (Winter 2000).

"Words of Hope and Warning: Diversity Is the Dominant Theme for the Class of '84." *Time* 123 (June 18, 1984): 75.

Zeiner, Dr. Helen Marsh. Review of *Beyond the Aspen Grove*. *Denver Botanical Garden Green Thumb* (Autumn 1970).

Zinsser, John. Review of audiotape of *The Mysterious Lands*. *Publishers Weekly* 240, no. 5 (February 1, 1993).

ACKNOWLEDGMENTS FOR "SHAPED BY WIND AND WATER"

by Ann Haymond Zwinger

My thanks to:

Emilie Buchwald and Scott Slovic, who shepherded this book with kind and firm hands and great patience and consideration;

Susan Zwinger, Jane Zwinger, and Sara Roberts, my admired, talented, and most respected daughters; I owe much to their stubborn patience and hard work to raise me into a reasonable adult (raising a parent gets more difficult every year); each read this manuscript at various stages and offered perceptive and helpful comments, not the least of which helped clear the cobwebs out of their mother's obfuscating style;

Sally Ann Roberts, named after her mother and grandmother, who reminds me of my obligations to tomorrow;

My first professor, Serapie der Nersessian, a Byzantine scholar who, during World War II, taught art history at Wellesley; she was never an "introductory teacher," although she taught the obligatory introductory class, but a woman of brilliance, clarity of mind, precision of statement. She, and Dr. Wilhelm Koehler, my professor in graduate school at Radcliffe/Harvard (who "stood up" with me when I was married), epitomized the ideals of scholarship and accuracy to which I aspire;

The scientific advisors who have kept me aware and accurate; many of them, in the midst of their own busy research and teaching schedules, took time to check my facts and guide my research; many read, commented on, and corrected portions of manuscripts, earning my undying gratitude;

Anne Cross, Joy Rucker, and Jo Boddington (and now Kathy Lowis), with whom I have had dinner monthly for sixteen years;

Ava Heinrichsdorff and Pat Musick, with whom I have breakfast every two weeks;

Timilou Rixon, who ballasts my syntax and sensibles my prose;

Karen Atkinson, organizer par excellence and wonderful working companion;

Julie Jones-Eddy, the world's most saintly (and competent) reference librarian;

Nancy Nordhoff, who made Hedgebrook possible, and Kim Berto, Linda Bowers, Cathy Breummer, Barton Cole, Beverly Graham, Ann Huggins, Denise Lee, Ella Peregine, Terrie Wallace, Sue Ellen White, the kindly, helpful people at Hedgebrook who make it so wonderful, and my companions there: Frances Lefkowitz, Nan Peacock, Carolyn Servid, and Tina Welling.

And lastly, my thanks to the admirable and lively women whose lives have enriched mine; it would be psychological suicide to attempt a list, so I must risk the hope that I have let them know of my affection and esteem through the years.

WORKS CITED

p. 3   Virginia Woolf, *A Writer's Diary*, ed.
           Leonard Woolf (London: Hogarth Press,
           1953), 26.

p. 17   Linda Hogan, *Dwellings: A Spiritual History
           of the Living World* (New York: Simon and
           Schuster, Touchstone, 1996), 60.

p. 20   Henry David Thoreau, *Thoreau on Birds:
           Notes on New England Birds from the Journals
           of Henry David Thoreau,* ed. Francis H.
           Allen (Boston: Beacon Press, 1993), 411.

p. 26   Frank Waters, *The Colorado* (New York:
           Rinehart and Company, 1946), 17.

p. 28   Edwin James, *Account of an Expedition from
           Pittsburgh to the Rocky Mountains,* vol. 2
           (London: Longman, Hurst, Rees, Orme,
           and Brown, 1823), 214.

p. 31   Beatrix Potter, *Beatrix Potter,* ed. Ruth K.
           MacDonald (Boston: Twayne Publishers,
           1986), 9.

p. 32   Helen Beach Cannon, "Stooping for Education," *High Country News* (April 24, 1989): 16.

p. 41   Rachel Carson, *Lost Woods: The Discovered Writing of Rachel Carson,* ed. Linda Lear (Boston: Beacon Press, 1998), 94, 95, 96.

p. 55   Beverly Graham, conversation with author, 1999.

p. 57   Virginia Woolf, *A Room of One's Own* (New York: Harcourt Brace Jovanovich, 1929), 4.

p. 63   Rachel Carson, *Speaking for Nature: How Literary Naturalists from Henry Thoreau to Rachel Carson Have Shaped America* by Paul Brooks (Boston: Houghton Mifflin Company, 1980), 286.

p. 64   Carson, *Speaking for Nature,* 286.

p. 69   Georgia O'Keeffe, *Georgia O'Keeffe* (New York: Viking Press, 1976).

p. 81   William Shakespeare, *As You Like It,* 2.1.15–17.

p. 82   William Wordsworth, "The Tables Turned," in *The Poetical Works of Wordsworth* (Boston: Houghton Mifflin, 1982), 830.

p. 83   Anne Morrow Lindbergh, *Gift from the Sea* (New York: Pantheon, 1955), 30, 50.

p. 89   Ann Zwinger and Edwin Way Teale, *A Conscious Stillness: Two Naturalists on*

Thoreau's Rivers (New York: Harper and Row, 1982), xviii.

p. 93   Ann Zwinger, *Beyond the Aspen Grove* (Tucson: University of Arizona Press, 1988), 142.

p. 94   Zwinger, *Beyond the Aspen Grove*, 8–9.

p. 95–96 Zwinger, *Beyond the Aspen Grove*, 19–20.

p. 102   Herman Zwinger, personal correspondence, January 5, 2000.

p. 103   Ann Zwinger and Beatrice E. Willard, *Land Above the Trees: A Guide to American Alpine Tundra* (New York: Harper and Row, 1972), viii.

p. 104   Zwinger and Willard, *Land Above the Trees*, 383.

p. 104   Edward Lueders, ed., *Writing Natural History: Dialogues with Authors* (Salt Lake City: University of Utah Press, 1989), 73.

p. 105   Ann Zwinger, personal correspondence, September 14, 1999.

p. 108   Susan Zwinger and Ann Zwinger, eds., *Women in Wilderness: Writings and Photographs* (San Diego: Tehabi, 1995), 9, 19.

p. 108–9 Ann Zwinger, *Downcanyon: A Naturalist Explores the Colorado River through the Grand Canyon* (Tucson: University of Arizona Press, 1995), 149.

p. 109–10 Henry David Thoreau, *Walden* (Boston: Beacon Press, 1997), 312.

p. 110 Ann Zwinger, personal correspondence, January 5, 2000.

SCOTT SLOVIC, founding president of the Association for the Study of Literature and Environment (ASLE), currently serves as editor of the journal *ISLE: Interdisciplinary Studies in Literature and Environment.* He is the author of *Seeking Awareness in American Nature Writing: Henry Thoreau, Annie Dillard, Edward Abbey, Wendell Berry, Barry Lopez* (University of Utah Press, 1992); his coedited books include *Being in the World: An Environmental Reader for Writers* (Macmillan, 1993), *Reading the Earth: New Directions in the Study of Literature and the Environment* (University of Idaho Press, 1998), and *Literature and the Environment: A Reader on Nature and Culture* (Addison Wesley Longman, 1999). Currently he is an associate professor of English and the director of the Center for Environmental Arts and Humanities at the University of Nevada, Reno.

Brown Dog of the Yaak:
Essays on Art and Activism
Rick Bass

Boundary Waters:
The Grace of the Wild
Paul Gruchow

Grass Roots:
The Universe of Home
Paul Gruchow

The Necessity of Empty Places
Paul Gruchow

A Sense of the Morning:
Field Notes of a Born Observer
David Brendan Hopes

Taking Care:
Thoughts on Storytelling and Belief
William Kittredge

The Barn at the End of the World:
The Apprenticeship of a Quaker, Buddhist Shepherd
Mary Rose O'Reilley

Walking the High Ridge:
Life As Field Trip
Robert Michael Pyle

Ecology of a Cracker Childhood
Janisse Ray

The Dream of the Marsh Wren:
Writing As Reciprocal Creation
Pattiann Rogers

The Country of Language
Scott Russell Sanders

Of Landscape and Longing:
Finding a Home at the Water's Edge
Carolyn Servid

The Book of the Tongass
Edited by Carolyn Servid and Donald Snow

Homestead
Annick Smith

Testimony:
Writers of the West Speak On Behalf of Utah Wilderness
Compiled by Stephen Trimble and
Terry Tempest Williams

Urban Nature:
Poems about Wildlife in the City
Edited by Laure-Anne Bosselaar

Verse and Universe:
Poems about Science and Mathematics
Edited by Kurt Brown

Poetry

Boxelder Bug Variations
Bill Holm

Butterfly Effect
Harry Humes

Eating Bread and Honey
Pattiann Rogers

Firekeeper:
New and Selected Poems
Pattiann Rogers

THE WORLD AS HOME, the nonfiction publishing program of Milkweed Editions, is dedicated to exploring our relationship to the natural world. Not espousing any particular environmentalist or political agenda, these books are a forum for distinctive literary writing that not only alerts the reader to vital issues but offers personal testimonies to living harmoniously with other species in urban, rural, and wilderness communities.

MILKWEED EDITIONS publishes with the intention of making a humane impact on society, in the belief that literature is a transformative art uniquely able to convey the essential experiences of the human heart and spirit. To that end, Milkweed publishes distinctive voices of literary merit in handsomely designed, visually dynamic books, exploring the ethical, cultural, and esthetic issues that free societies need continually to address. Milkweed Editions is a not-for-profit press.

Typeset in Stone Serif
by Stanton Publication Services, Inc.
Printed on acid-free, recycled
55# Frasier Miami Book Natural paper
by Friesen Corporation.